THE
LION OF
SABRAY

THE AFGHANI WARRIOR
WHO DEFIED THE TALIBAN AND SAVED
THE LIFE OF NAVY SEAL MARCUS LUTTRELL

PATRICK ROBINSON

Touchstone

New York London Toronto Sydney New Delhi

Touchstone
An Imprint of Simon & Schuster, Inc.
1230 Avenue of the Americas
New York, NY 10020

First Touchstone hardcover edition November 2015

TOUCHSTONE and colophon are registered trademarks of Simon & Schuster, Inc.

For information about special discounts for bulk purchases, please contact Simon & Schuster Special Sales at 1-866-506-1949 or business@simonandschuster.com.

The Simon & Schuster Speakers Bureau can bring authors to your live event. For more information or to book an event, contact the Simon & Schuster Speakers Bureau at 866-248-3049 or visit our website at www.simonspeakers.com.

Interior design by Jill Putorti

All photographs by Nawaz Rahini

Manufactured in the United States of America

10   9   8   7   6   5   4   3   2   1

Library of Congress Cataloging-in-Publication Data

Robinson, Patrick, 1939-
  The Lion of Sabray : the Afghani warrior who defied the Taliban and saved the life of Navy Seal Marcus Luttrell / by Patrick Robinson.
    pages cm
  1. Gulab, Mohammed. 2. Luttrell, Marcus. 3. Afghan War, 2001—Biography. 4. Rescues—Afghanistan—History—21st century. 5. Honor—Afghanistan—Case studies. 6. Pushtuns—Afghanistan—Biography. 7. Soldiers—Afghanistan—Biography. 8. United States. Navy. SEALs—Biography. 9. Soldiers—United States—Biography. I. Title.
  DS371.43.G85R62 2015
  958.104'7092—dc23
  [B]
                                                                      2015009149

ISBN 978-1-5011-1798-5
ISBN 978-1-5011-1800-5 (ebook)

For every one of the decent village warriors
who saved the life of my buddy Marcus.

CONTENTS

NOTE FROM MOHAMMED GULAB

When I discovered the wounded American soldier Marcus Luttrell outside my village, I had no idea how that moment would forever change the course of my life, my family's life, and affect the lives of everyone in our village high up in the mountains of Afghanistan. But God spoke to me that day and said I must give protection to this man; that he fell under the Pashtunwali rules that guide our lives. Marcus Luttrell is a great warrior, and I am filled with love and respect for the man. I am happy that we were able to give him aid and help in his rescue. Even with all the hardship that has followed. This is my story and the story of those eventful days. I hope it finds you well.

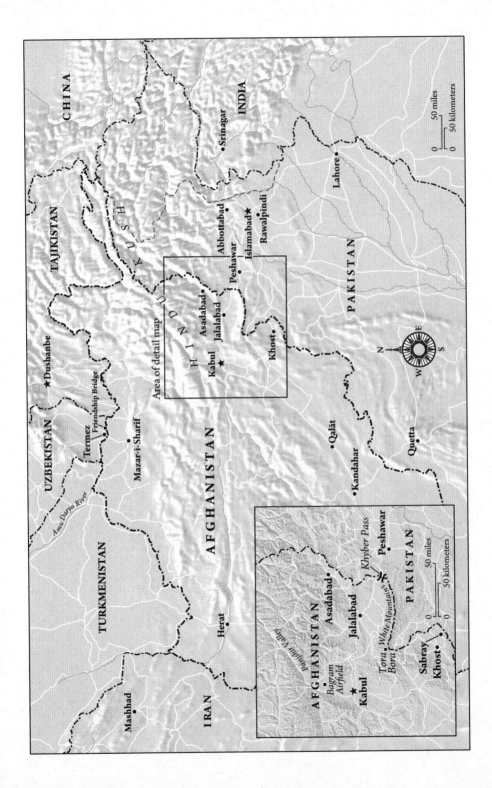

PROLOGUE

Mohammed Gulab is a Pashtun tribesman. A mountain man. His people are a remote group who've lived for millenniums in the high peaks of the Hindu Kush located in the back end of the Himalayas, on the uncharted borders of Pakistan, Uzbekistan, Tajikistan, and what some Westerners might feel is God-knows-wherever-else-istan.

Their language is a specific dialect, evolved from the ancient tribal tongue of Afghanistan. More than three hundred years before Christ. The Macedonian, Alexander the Great, chatted away to them with the ease of a would-be conqueror. Today these people are understood only in the city of Jalalabad, never mind in the Western world.

Mohammed Gulab's heritage is, shall we say, hazy. He has no birth certificate. His official entry into this world was not even recorded.

I'm not sure the birth of any of his ancestors has ever been recorded; not up there in those distant, high peaks, where the Pashtuns have lived and died for thousands of years.

He believes he was born in 1973. There is no benchmark except for the oldest brother, Haji Nazer Gul, who was born sixteen years previously—but, again, not recorded.

They named him Mohammed Gulab. It might have been Mohammed Gulab Gulab. But either way, his name is Gulab. No one ever called him anything else, at least not among his friends and family. Gulab is closely related to the tribal elder in a village that clings to the edge of a towering mountain on a gradient only slightly steeper than the Washington Monument. Encounters with people from the West are, naturally, limited.

So it is particularly remarkable that Gulab's experiences include the unlikely lifelong, binding association with a very special US Navy SEAL, Marcus Luttrell, who asserts flatly that but for Gulab, he would have died on an Afghan mountain in June 2005, along with his best friend and eighteen other US Special Forces.

Marcus was part of a SEALs mission to capture or kill one Mullah Ahmad Shah, a notorious Taliban terrorist believed to have recently blown up a truckload of US Marines. (For this book, I have elected to switch to the classified correct name of the Taliban commander. So many people have revealed the name, and the Taliban leader whom Marcus describes as "that evil little sonofabitch" is dead now, anyway. I checked with SEAL Command, and there is no longer any issue.)

PROLOGUE

The armed Americans had been deposited onto Gulab's mountains as a small US Special Force. The four SEALs were scattered around a little stony ridge where they had made their command center, overlooking Shah's digs about a half mile below. Danny was on comms, Axe on guard, Mikey on glass, Marcus with the sniper rifle. But before they could complete their mission, they were confronted by goat-herders, one of them just a kid aged about fourteen, who'd come upon the SEALs unawares.

The story of what happened next is well known by fans of *Lone Survivor*. To kill or not to kill? Marcus Luttrell understood implicitly the danger of releasing local tribesmen who might even be members of the Taliban—informers, spies, or perhaps relatives of recruited warriors. With or without the goats, they could be in that Taliban camp in a heartbeat, informing Shah that they'd just met four heavily armed American combatants. But could they just stand here, raise their rifles, and kill an unarmed teenager? The SEALs were all Christians, all with Christian souls, and the question stood stark before Mikey and Marcus: Would God ever forgive them for such a deed?

I know Marcus Luttrell better than most people, having written *Lone Survivor* with him. And if it makes anyone feel any wiser, I should say that those moments, and that decision to free the goat-herders, have haunted him ever since. There still aren't many nights he doesn't wake up trembling at the thought of it all and what it ultimately meant both to him and, more importantly, to his buddies.

Of course, the goat-herders charged straight to Shah's army with their information. But was the SEALs' decision right or wrong? Who can say? Marcus says, "All I do know is that if we'd voted the other way, Axe, Danny, and Mikey would be alive today, and if you want to break my heart more than it is already, just remind me of that."

As the SEALs moved away from the Taliban encampment, Marcus saw a bearded Al Qaeda killer behind a tree, carefully drawing a bead on him. The Afghani's AK-47 was aimed straight at Marcus's forehead. It was the tribesman or him, and Marcus squeezed the trigger.

The shot echoed around the mountain. And then all hell broke loose. After an incredibly brave stand against a Taliban army numbering as many as four hundred strong, the four Americans' luck ran out. Danny was killed; Axe, probably dying; Mikey, shot in the stomach; and Marcus—battered half to death—had nowhere to turn.

For the only time in his life, he heard the voice of God. He has thought of that moment often. And there has never been one shred of doubt in his mind. The voice was deep and clear. His God had reached down and given Marcus hope. Of that he was certain. That was when he knew somehow that he was not alone, and then he turned to face the enemy once more with a newfound confidence. And, privately, he thanked God Almighty for giving him that chance.

Marcus kept telling himself over and over, *"I'm a SEAL. And I still believe we have a chance. I still have my rifle, loaded. And somehow, deep in my heart, I believe God knows that, and He is still in my corner."*

Only a lunatic, or perhaps a SEAL team leader, possibly could have viewed the overall position of the three surviving Redwings as anything beyond hopeless. Mikey had been shot again, and Axe had a deadly head wound. Aside from a left leg full of shrapnel and rock chips, and a bloodied face, Marcus might have looked and felt a bit better than his buddies, but not by much.

The trouble was, there seemed to be just as many against them as there had been at the start. They'd lost all form of comms, except for Mikey's cell phone, which could not get transmission, jammed against this towering granite rock face that blocked out east, north, and west.

But then Lieutenant Mike Murphy made a decision. Blood-soaked, grim-faced, he stepped out into the clearing to where there was likely more of a signal, and, taking out his cell phone, he called for help. "My men are taking heavy fire. . . . We're getting picked apart. My guys are dying out here. We need help."

All three SEALs understood that he was sacrificing his life. As the SEAL officer in charge, however, nothing would prevent him from doing his duty.

Right then a bullet hit him straight in the back. And with bullets still flying all around him and blood pouring, he spoke one final sentence: "Roger that, sir. Thank you."

A powerful rocket grenade blasted Marcus out of the hollow, across the rough terrain and over some kind of a ravine, knocking him unconscious. When he came around, he was blind—couldn't see a thing. He was also upside down—everything hurting like hell—headfirst in a hole. Somehow he hauled himself out and found himself in sunlight, with vision intact. The only thing he could see was his miracle of a rifle, right there, a couple of feet from his hand, as he exited the hole.

"In my own mind, I was now entirely on my own," he reflected later. "This Taliban army was no longer searching for a SEAL team. It was trying to hunt down me alone."

By any reasonable calculation, Marcus had zero chance. His leg, full of fragmented metal, felt paralyzed. His pants had been blown right off, he was suffering from a serious loss of blood, and there was a definite possibility he might die of thirst. The one shred of good news was that the enemy couldn't see him. A thousand bullets had missed Marcus that afternoon, and his faith was still strong. God did not wish him to die here today, on this desperate foreign mountain. Marcus knew he had to move into better cover. Suddenly the enemy opened up fire again, bullets flashing into this rough ground from all over the place.

For Shah, the great triumph of the afternoon had come when the US military had sent in a Chinook helicopter, packed with reinforcements, to rescue any of the four who might still be alive. The Taliban missile men had brought that Chinook down, killing all sixteen on board.

Marcus was resolved, still, to find water, and continue his crablike progress across the face of this mountain. The pain in his leg was by now devastating. He'd had nothing to drink for a total of fourteen hours. He was light-headed, drifting between reality and hallucination.

As for the downed Chinook, Marcus would not know it had happened for several days, which was just as well, because reports of the tragic deaths of his close friends like Shane, James, Jeff, Erik, and Chief Dan, all trying to save him, might easily have sent him over the edge into insanity. Only later would he learn that when Mikey's last, desperate phone call came through at the SEAL base—"My guys are dying"—the Quick Reaction Force hit the blacktop faster than ever before, scrambling into the Chinook, pulling on their gear, magazines snapping into position. Forty minutes after takeoff, everyone on board was dead. It was the worst day in the history of the US Navy SEALs.

In order to elude the Taliban, Marcus made one final diabolical crash down the Afghan mountain. His left leg had taken enough punishment for one lifetime and it finally buckled completely, sending him into a headlong fall. He shot past a deep pool below a waterfall at about seventy miles per hour, going straight down, no brakes, no steering.

The impact was stunning. He lay there for a while, eyes closed, feeling just about as sorry for himself as it was possible to be. Then, slowly, he tried to move, testing arms and legs, checking whether anything still worked. To his utter amazement, pretty much everything was in order, and, amazingly, his rifle had landed just a foot away. He grabbed, dug, and clawed his way up. It took about two hours to reach the waterfall. In some kind of desperate effort, he got there, scuffling over the final yards, and then he just plunged his head in. No water, he says, ever had, or ever will, taste that sweet.

He then lay there in tears, thanking God, his savior, and begging the Almighty not to abandon him, because without that merciful hand, Marcus could not have survived.

That merciful hand came in the form of Mohammed Gulab. Marcus has always been, typically, the very soul of generosity in his gratitude to Gulab. He once told me, "In the seven days following the battle, I could have died about nine more deaths. Gulab saved me, and on every occasion, he put his own life on the line, facing down inevitable death himself. Without him, I'd be in a coffin."

The truth was, in a blink of Gulab's dark eyes, Marcus's enemies became his own. Gulab chose to defend and shelter the "infidel": this gravely injured Navy SEAL. The Al Qaeda tribal killers, seeking to gun down the American, would probably have mutilated Luttrell's face, as they'd done to Mikey, Danny, and Axe.

Outside of Marcus's own valorous SEAL community, he swears that Mohammed Gulab is the bravest man he's ever known, though theirs would be a friendship founded on a higher awareness—an unspoken sense of empathy. Gulab could not read or write even in his own language, and he would never learn English, as Marcus would never learn the Pashtun's ancient tribal dialect. Since their fateful first encounter on the mountain, Gulab and Marcus have each made thousands of hand signals, one to the other.

They've had translators, interpreters, they've mimed, play-acted, and laughed. But they have never shared an understood word.

The man to whom Marcus Luttrell owes the most in all the world is ultimately silent to him. He does not even know the name of his wife, or the names of his ten children. But they are often in each other's thoughts, even half a world away.

So much of what they both feel can never be said—will never be said. Neither of them knows how to mime words such as *loyalty, concern,* and *anxiety.* Mohammed Gulab will always stand as a pillar in the life of Marcus and his family. Gulab was once an assumed enemy, but became a devoted friend.

He and Marcus were born eight thousand miles apart, separated by every possible shred of human learning, instinct, and religion. But those days on the mountain flung them together, and the vast distances of their lives can never cast them asunder.

Through an interpreter, Gulab speaks of Marcus with unmistakable compassion, like a slightly older brother smiling at the memories of long-lost sharing.

In the ensuing years after the publication of *Lone Survivor*, I have been asked this more than any other question: What happened to the tribesman who saved Marcus, and did Marcus and the tribesman ever meet again?

People were haunted by the heartbreaking picture of Marcus banging on the cockpit glass, yelling at the pilot to wait—and Gulab's tearful, anguished face as the military rescue helicopter rose up and left him behind on the Asadabad runway.

In that awful moment, Mohammed Gulab became, effectively, stateless. He could not go home. He was an outcast among many of his own people: the man who had saved the infidel. And America appeared to have abandoned him.

High above, flying through the peaks of the Hindu Kush toward safety, Marcus Luttrell was outraged at this treatment of his personal savior. And it took years for the two men to find each other again.

When they finally did, in Texas, I flew to meet them, to begin work on the book that would answer two important questions: Who exactly was the tribesman? And what happened to him?

PASHTUNWALI

The Pashtuns are a fiercely independent people who have inhabited Afghanistan since at least 1000 BC on steep mountainous terrain, completely outside government control or rule. They have their own laws, and no one is advised to try to force a different way of life upon them. Government committees and even the Taliban in both Pakistan and Afghanistan understand that Pashtun laws *must* be accepted in the Hindu Kush mountains. The Pashtuns have their ways, and there are forty-two million of them worldwide, twenty-eight million in Afghanistan. If necessary, every one of them would rally to defend the honor of those laws.

The codes of Pashtunwali are not inscribed upon parchment. They are handed down from pre-Islamic times, but they work in concert with the teachings of the Prophet Muhammad. They contain all ten main principles that Pashtun tribesmen adhere to:

1. *Melmastia* (hospitality). Hospitality and deep respect are extended to all visitors, regardless of race, religion, national affiliation, or economic status. And done so without any hope of remuneration or favor.

2. *Nanawateh* (asylum). This refers to protection given to a person against his enemies. People—visitors—must be protected at all costs. Even those running from the law must be given refuge until the situation can be clarified.

3. *Badal* (justice). There is no time limit on seeking justice or taking revenge against a wrongdoer. In Pashtun lore, even a simple taunt (*paighor*) is regarded as an insult, which usually is rectified by the shedding of blood. If the culprit cannot be located, his closest male relative must suffer the penalty instead. *Badal* can lead to blood feuds that may last generations, involve entire tribes, and cost hundreds of lives.

4. *Tureh* (bravery). A Pashtun must forever defend his land, property, family, and women from invasion. He will stand bravely against tyranny, and defend the honor of his name. Death may follow if anyone offends this principle.

5. *Sabat* (loyalty). Loyalty must be paid to one's family, friends, and tribe members. Disloyalty cannot be tolerated, for it brings profound shame on both families and individuals.

6. *Imandari* (righteousness). All Pashtuns must strive for good,

in thought, word, and deed. They must behave respectfully to people, animals, and the environment around them. All pollution of the environment, or its destruction, is a direct affront to Pashtunwali.

7. *Isteqamat* (trust in God—*Allah* in Arabic, *Khudai* in ancient Pashto). To trust in the one and only Creator parallels the Islamic certainty that there is only one God *(Tawheed)*.

8. *Ghayrat* (courage). Pashtuns must *demonstrate* courage. Their honor and pride has enormous importance in Pashtun society and must be preserved. Respect for others is paramount; respect for family, automatic. A lack of this brand of prideful *ghayrat* can mean exile.

9. *Namus* (protection of women). A Pashtun must defend the honor of women at any and all cost; protection from vocal and physical harm.

10. *Nang* (honor). A Pashtun *must* defend the weak around him.

A TRIBAL WARRIOR IS BORN

When the late Lieutenant General Mikhail Kalashnikov made the final refinements to his universal assault rifle back in the 1960s, he became a patron saint of revolution. In the decades following the new production lines for the AK-47, the sixty-year-old Mikhail armed just about every disgruntled terror group on the planet.

From half-educated jihadists and the armies of rogue states to crazed Far Eastern dictators and jack-booted communist secret police. The "Kalash," as the Russians call it, has armed millions of malcontents, from Red China to the Congo, from North Korea to Baghdad, from Beirut to Tehran and back.

Of course, it also armed the Red Army, and it was the mainstay of the army of Afghani Patriots, the mujahideen, whose country was invaded by the Soviet Union in 1979.

In the past, everyone was drawn to the AK's gas-driven rotating bolt rifle, the cyclic six-hundred-rounds-per-minute firing rate, the four-hundred-meter range, and, of course, its famous reliability, durability, and availability. The old Soviets would sell that weapon to anyone.

The rifle was heavy. With its sturdy wooden stock, it weighed almost ten pounds with the magazine loaded, but it had a back-kick like an angry mule, which often resulted in bullets being sprayed around all over the place by would-be warriors with weak wrists—men who could scarcely hit a barn door at point-blank range.

But complaints were few. And even the genuine gripe of the home guerilla army in Afghanistan, fighting the invading Russians in the deep valleys of the Hindu Kush, quickly accepted that Mikhail's masterpiece had a flaw: it was utterly unsuitable as the weapon of choice for the youngest mujahideen recruits, who were often around eight years old. The fact was, it was too heavy, too much of a handful, too much gun.

The mujahideen treasure their boy soldiers, the armies of the future. And local commanders expected everyone to be battle-trained by the time he reached the age of twelve. And, of course, the first great skill they needed to learn was to shoot straight.

With no birth certificates, this was all slightly hit-or-miss when assessing the kids for active infantry duty against the Red Army.

When he was eight, Gulab was taken away from his village to fight the Russians. He was small for his age and could hardly lift the Kalashnikov.

He struggled to raise it while peering down the adjustable iron sight. He pulled the trigger fast, just in case he dropped it and killed one of his own side. That rifle slammed against his shoulder and knocked him flat on his back.

The 7.62-millimeter bullet could have gone anywhere, and before he climbed back to his feet, one of the junior commanders gave him a sharp slap across the face, presumably for military incompetence. It was some years before they ordered him once more to carry the standard mujahideen assault rifle.

This was not, however, a problem to be solved by sending him home to his village, back to school, or to his studies of the Koran. Gulab was here on the battlefield, the younger brother of one of the mujahideens' finest commanders, and if he was too small for the Kalash, they'd find him something else to fire on the enemy. Age was not an issue.

To a Westerner, it does seem cruel to hear of children being recruited for a ferocious and historic tribal army pledged to fight to the death for its hilly homeland. But fighting is just a way of life in their culture, and Gulab will confirm endlessly that it was not strange for him, nor for his family. And at the time, they were at war with invaders. There was no other life. Gulab comes from a Pashtun tribe. Mountain men and women. His tiny village, high in the Himalayas, has always been under attack, from gangsters, smugglers, thieves, warlords, and, more recently, Al Qaeda, the Taliban sect who covet the seclusion, and other rival factions who covet the lush, timbered slopes and relatively prosperous way of living.

Gulab speaks thoughtfully about his own birthplace. "Sabray is just a little village," he says. "And I suppose a Westerner might consider it a primitive place. There are only two houses which have an iron stove in which to bake our bread, and this we share every day. Our electricity supply is limited to one generator, and water comes from a mountain river.

"Sabray is built on a steep gradient, well over three thousand feet above sea level in the Hindu Kush range, with peaks towering many thousands of feet above us all. Sounds echo across the valleys, bouncing off the walls of the mountains."

The village stands slightly north of the world's 33rd parallel, in Central Asia, in a time zone nine and a half hours ahead of the East Coast of the United States.

It's close to the Pakistan border, and 135 miles from the Afghan capital of Kabul, which lies across high mountains and seems like half a world away if you're walking, as most Afghanis do.

For centuries, the people of Sabray have fought like lions for what they owned. There was a family Kalashnikov always ready in the main room of every house, magazine clipped and loaded. Everyone carries a tribal knife. Thieves are likely to meet a quick end.

If the men are away working, the women are equally dangerous. The chances of any thief getting out of any house with his life intact are remote. The Pashtuns traditionally shoot to kill and, if necessary, deliver the precision slash to the throat from an Afghan tribal knife.

"Every house and family in the village is similar," says Gulab. "The citizens of Sabray are renowned throughout Kunar Province as fighters, fearless soldiers, skilled in the art of war. Men from Sabray have long been considered the very heart of the mountain armies. It is often said that a hundred thirty warriors from Sabray will seem like ten thousand to any enemy."

US Special Forces will confirm how these mountain men move swiftly, silently, and ruthlessly. They are experts at moving over every inch of those rocky, barely charted escarpments. They have never cared for outright confrontation with the fire and steel of any occupying army, like those of Great Britain (nineteenth century), the Soviet Union (1980 to 1989), or the United States (now). Their specialty is ambush. And no one is too young to learn that.

Which is, more or less, why young Gulab was marched off to war at such an early age and why such high expectations were leveled upon him.

He still recalls the moment when he was flung to the ground by the kick-back of that AK-47. "The incident ran close to a family disgrace," he said, frowning at the memory. "I was not aware of it at the time, but I was aware of the immense reputation of my brother, Commander Nazer Gul, a very, very dangerous man.

"Eighteen times he'd been wounded in battle. And eighteen times, he fought back to resume his command. Gul is a trained killer, once jailed for twenty years for ending the life of a tribal enemy. In fact, they let him out after only five years, on the simple condition that he immediately raise a mujahideen army of Sabray fighters—men everyone knew would follow him into hell."

His mission was to train them and join in the mujahideens' fight against the occupying Russians. By the time Gulab arrived on those treacherous high peaks, Gul was one of the senior officers.

"I'm not sure he ever knew his kid brother had been flattened by my own rifle," says Gulab. "But I do know an order came down from very high up that I was to be inducted immediately into guerilla warfare using a more manageable weapon."

For this the Afghanis chose the heavy, lethal Soviet machine gun the DShK-38 (the Russians call it the *dushka*), with its huge 12.7-millimeter cartridge, two-thousand-meter range, fifty-round ammunition belt, armor-plated shield, and heavy-wheeled mounting. The gun alone weighed seventy-five pounds and, once, handled erratically by the Irish Republican Army, knocked a six-ton British army Westland Lynx helicopter clean out of the sky and dumped it on the shores of the Cashel Lough in County Armagh.

The eight-year-old Gulab could not believe the size of it when they led him to the machine gun station. The good news was that he did not have to lift it. The bad news was that he could not reach it to look through the crosshairs.

The DShK-38 was in a fixed firing position, its three-prong stand jammed into the ground, and they had to get Gulab up there somehow. Huge, flat stones were collected to build a platform for him to stand on and start blasting away with one of the most deadly large-caliber weapons in the world. It shook like hell, but it did not kick back like the Kalash. And Gulab remembers enjoying himself, banging away at distant rocks and trees. His teachers were right: it was a lot easier to handle than a Russian infantry assault rifle.

What led to Gulab being attached to that machine gun were the momentous events of December 25, 1979, when the Red Army marched into Afghanistan from the north and attempted to subjugate the people to the unwanted purposes of the Soviet Union, under the leadership of President Leonid Brezhnev.

Gulab was about six years old at the time and not aware of the significance of that invasion. In fact, it took some time for the nation to understand precisely what had happened and what it might mean. But there was a very definite sense of consternation, and there were meetings of the village elders and a call to arms was issued by the mujahideen.

It was the first time Gulab ever experienced mass tension in the village. He knew that his brother Haji Nazer Gul was "away" but was never told he was in jail for murder. And he does recall his return, liberated by the authorities in order to lead the men of Sabray into battle. He scarcely understood that the mujahideen would fight, and keep fighting, until the Russians marched right back out of Afghanistan and stayed out.

At the age of six, Gulab might not have been totally focused, but he understood the word *enemy*—and everyone knew there was an enemy close by. They did not know exactly what he wanted, or why he was there, but they did know he worshipped a different God and therefore was an infidel. Abstractly, the villagers knew that the tribesmen would, in time, defeat the Russians and drive them away. Equally vaguely, every young man in the community understood that he would be required to fight in the not-too-distant future.

The daily prayers in the village mosque contained a heightened awareness of the battles that loomed ahead, and they recited the eternal cry of the Islamic creed: *"La Ilaha ill Allah Muhammadur-Rasul Allah"*: "There is no god but Allah. Muhammad is the messenger of Allah."

Other new but ancient words also echoed throughout the village, and that translation read: "Oh, God. Please make us successful in our fight. Please help us to kill the infidel. May God bless us." The learned men drilled it into those very young minds.

The words were simple, and they were part of the prayers offered five times a day, beginning at dawn and right through to sundown. And every single time, when the gathering turned to face Mecca, in Saudi Arabia, the village elders and the learned men prayed with the Imam; prayed for a just victory over the intruders from the North.

This was the mantra for Islamic life, even for those so young. The senior men frequently went to war and frequently came back. But not always. Gulab understood swiftly that friends had lost fathers and brothers in the Russian conflict. They all knew the dangers and understood the risks. They knew that the children, too, would one day follow them out onto the steep, dusty slopes of guerilla warfare, where they would kill to survive, as their ancestors had always done.

For the people of Sabray, the tradition of "blooding" boy soldiers to join the line of battle in the Hindu Kush was as timeless as life itself. It's entirely foreign to Western culture. But Gulab found nothing strange in it. The right to fight and kill an invading enemy is instilled in Pashtun culture.

Every young boy was taught the last great triumph of the tribal warriors of Afghanistan: how the bearded Islamists had destroyed the British army in the infamous retreat from Kabul in January 1842. Everyone was taught how the English major general Sir William Elphinstone, attempting an orderly retreat out of Afghanistan, was wiped out in the mountain passes. Out of sixteen thousand men, only one made it home to the garrison in India. The last stand of the British was made in the Gandamak Pass along the road from Kabul, when those renowned veterans of Waterloo, the Forty-Fourth Regiment of Foot (the Fighting Fours of Essex), were annihilated by Afghan warriors, fighting from the heights.

The Afghanis were the supreme exponents of ambush combat. One hundred fifty years later, Britain's *Spectator* magazine described that combat as an "almost perfect catastrophe." As it was then, so it will always be: the ancient Afghan promise of "You try to conquer us, in the end you die."

That British retreat is known in the Hindu Kush as the Massacre of Elphinstone's Army. And it should be said that the Forty-Fourth

Regiment fought back with great gallantry to the last man, refusing to surrender despite British losses of 4,500 troops and almost 12,000 civilian workers, family members, and camp followers.

All nations are formed by their history and their heroes of the past. And the Pashtuns were most certainly created by theirs. From their earliest years, the village teaching was simple: *We may be attacked, we may even be conquered, but we will always fight back, and we will never give up. . . . We battle, if necessary, until there is no one left. If we run out of ammunition, we will use our rifles as clubs, and if we run out of rifles, we will resort to our tribal knives, and night after night we will cut the throats of our enemies, until they leave our territory.*

Gulab became very confident with the Russian dushka, and in the coming eight years of warfare, he was recognized quickly as a master gunner, firing the mounted heavy machine gun with precision. The very young learn very easily. In Afghanistan, that's especially important.

Back in the village, they heard the outbreak of the Russian war from the sustained gunfire out of a deep valley, about eleven miles away across the mountains.

The sounds of that first battle had a pattern: long, drawn-out gun bursts, short and sharp at first; and then louder, more serious, as the mujahideen commanders switched to the heavy machine guns, firing on the Russians from the high walls of the valley. In the end, there would be, possibly, four massive explosions, like detonating a mountainside, and then a strong, shuddering, lingering aftershock. Then silence.

Long before his eighth birthday, Gulab knew what those sounds represented, though it took him several weeks as a junior machine gunner to understand the most important part of mujahideen strategy. This occurred in the hours of profound silence that preceded an Afghan opening attack.

These were the hours when the mujahideen commanders ordered battle lines into position. The ambush site had been selected, always above a valley being approached by a large Russian convoy. The mountain warriors moved swiftly and quietly up to the heights, crossing their native ground, utilizing the "dead spots" behind rocks and trees, from where they could not be seen from the valley below.

The first time Gulab saw them, it was like watching shadows: these brave, fearless tribesmen moving across the shifting shale escarpments, leaving scarcely even a footprint and certainly not causing any sand or rock to slip down the steep slopes. He once told me, somewhat sardonically, "Anyone can do it like us—after about two thousand years of practice!"

No enemy of Afghanistan has training like the natives. Certainly not the Russians, nor the Brits nor the Americans. Those mountains are the mujahideen training grounds; all their lives are spent moving across them, making no sounds, because of the endless dangers. Gulab remembers his first battle. It took many hours to prepare firing positions, and then they waited, high above the valley floor, with no one making a sound.

"Mostly," he told me, "I remember my brother Haji Nazer Gul. Sometimes he was the only man moving, making signals, checking ammunition belts, adjusting aim-and-fire placements, always with his big Russian rifle slung over his shoulder.

"When, at last, he was finished, we could see him above us, in conference with the senior commanders, while our lookouts—positioned high on the rocks—stared down into the valley, searching for the dust cloud, which swirled inevitably above the Russian convoy.

"As soon as they came rumbling into the valley, with no escape, neither to the left nor right, our orders were simple. Upon the command, we would open fire on the armored vehicle drivers and commanders—those we could see clearly. They could not, of course, see us, since we were ducked down behind huge boulders a long way above them."

Mujahideen strategy was to level sustained fire down on the enemy, concentrating on the rearguard, and thus driving the leaders forward to the end of the valley. And there the Afghanis finished them with their biggest bombs, planted in booby-trap order, sometimes in the valley floor. Often there were few survivors.

Once, in a summer ambush, Gulab was in a strange quietness from the shattered convoy. And then, as the commanders walked down to finish off any still-breathing Russians, he recalls a huge black cloud rising from the bodies, way up into the sky, blotting out the sun. This was a flock of crows—looked like millions and millions of them—feeding off the corpses. It was absolutely horrible.

And for the first time in his young life, he thought war was a really terrible business. "Up till then," he said, "I thought it had something to do with heroism."

The Russians considered those ruthless ambushes barbaric, but the mountain men don't really go much for subtlety. They go for death, especially to the infidel. And if the Russians did not like it, well, perhaps they should have thought about that before they invaded the ancient Islamic homeland of the Pashtun people.

It worked against the earlier British invaders and it would work again against the Russians. The mujahideen were perfectly willing to face death. And they could melt into those mountains, invisible in an instant. Pursuit was impossible.

The war had been going on for about a year when Gulab was first called to the front line. The timeline began on the Christians' holy day of December 25, when the Russians staged a massive military airlift into Kabul. It involved nearly three hundred transport aircraft and more than twenty-five thousand men, and after a savage battle in the city, they took the Tajbeg Palace. Kabul fell.

Simultaneously, Russian tanks rolled out of the ancient Uzbekistan city of Termez, which was no stranger to war, having been conquered by Alexander the Great in 329 BC, and then, more than 1,500 years later, destroyed by Genghis Khan. In that wild northern territory, the Amu Dar'ya River divides the two countries, Uzbekistan and Afghanistan. The bridge across those swiftly flowing mountain waters is called the Friendship Bridge, but it should have been renamed. In the decade after the Soviet attack, more than a hundred thousand Russian soldiers marched out of their Termez military headquarters and over that highway, heading south into hostile Afghan mountains.

Whatever Mr. Brezhnev said about supporting the Kabul government, there was nothing friendly about his armies. And their ultimate fate was sealed very early in 1980.

The mujahideen, the historic jihadist army, declared that the Russian invaders had defiled both Islam and Afghani culture. And they immediately declared jihad, citing the literal meaning of that old Arab word: "struggle." And they vowed to go on killing the Soviets until they left.

This was a holy war, and they conducted it fiercely, in the name of Allah, reviving the nineteenth-century creed of the iron-souled mujahideen tribesmen who massacred the forces of General Elphinstone.

Communications in the valleys of Kunar Province were limited, but in the ancient ways of the Pashtun tribes, the call to arms flashed through the high peaks, man to man, village to village, like a kind of tribal bush telegraph. Gulab was not yet seven years old, but he still remembers the men of Sabray gathering their rifles and leaving together, many of them led by his own brother.

It was fitting somehow that the conflict's very first battle was fought in a valley not eleven miles from his village. He was always told the mujahideen won it, but even at his tender age, he already understood that the men of Sabray would never admit defeat no matter what the outcome really was.

And from that moment, in the opening days of the Christian New Year, the Russians would meet ferocious resistance all along the main Kunar road that runs along the river. In fact, the Russians ran into heavy-handed opposition whenever they ventured out of their city strongholds and into the countryside. And they probably never understood why the men of the mujahideen fought with such venom.

The truth was, they had to win those early skirmishes for one practical reason: the mujahideen needed to grab the Russian weapons and the explosives. There was no way to buy them, so they had to be stolen in battle. And the tribesmen did not care how many of the enemy they killed—anything to get those rifles, machine guns, hand grenades, rockets, and bombs.

They never took tanks or armored vehicles, because they were useless in the steep-walled valleys, and anyway, the mountain men were not sure how to work them. They usually just blew them up with the Russians' own high explosives, on the basis that if the tribesmen couldn't use them, neither could the occupying army.

The mujahideen stuck rigidly to the strategies of guerilla warfare: ambush and surprise attacks, plus murderous assaults on the enemy guards and young officers in the dead of night. No training was needed for this.

Gulab estimates that he was called in 1981. By that time, the Russians had taken some bad losses and in many ways were already on the run, especially out in the wild country, where they were hit hard over and over. Once he had recovered from being flattened by the AK-47, Gulab moved up onto his platform of mountain granite and began work as a gunner.

This was his first job, and once he mastered the terrific vibration of the dushka, he was able to aim it pretty well. After a three-day walk from Sabray, they positioned themselves high up over a valley, on both sides. The heavy machine guns were already in place, the barrels aimed down at the road through the central pass. Behind just one of them, the flat stones awaited him, and they made camp up there in the hills and waited.

They waited maybe for two days until the lookouts signaled that the Russian convoy was coming. There was huge excitement, but no one spoke. The commanders moved among the gunners, checking ammunition supplies. Gulab kept very still up there; at one point, his brother came by and told him to fire steady when the time arrived.

Everyone saw the leading Russian tanks and trucks come rumbling into the valley, and the mujahideen commanders let them get well entrenched between the rock faces before ordering the Afghan riflemen to open up, pouring volley after volley into the convoy.

They could see the armored vehicles swerving, trying to get away from the fire. But then Commander Haji Nazer Gul ordered the dushkas to start shooting. "For the first time," said Gulab, "in the anger of battle, aged eight, I hit the trigger."

Gulab recounts that opening action of the Russian war:

I could tell my big shells were slamming into the vehicles I aimed at, but very quickly a great cloud of dust was surrounding them, and I thought I'd better stop wasting ammunition, since I could no longer see what I was shooting at.

That was one of my earliest military errors. There was a sporadic return of fire from Russian troops, who had got free of their tanks, and I could tell there were bullets hitting the dusty terrain around me and ricocheting off the rocks.

Up on the higher slopes, where a line of our machine gunners worked, there were several big explosions, with shale and sand being hurled down over our heads. Nothing hit me, but I was covered in dust and feeling a bit bewildered.

But right then, Haji Nazer Gul yelled at me to get behind the iron shield on my dushka and keep firing no matter what: *"Fire into the dust cloud! Don't let them think they have cover! Keep banging away until there's no one left alive!"* And that's what I did. If something or someone moved, I blasted it—I knew my high-caliber bullets could cut a man in half, and I just kept blazing away into the melee below.

"Keep firing, kid! Hold your position!"

By now, I had learned the chilling battle cry of the mujahideen, a loud, echoing roar, which sounded like a scream from the mouth of hell. It was designed to strike fear into the hearts of the enemy, and from all accounts, that's what it did. I loved it, and even though my voice had not yet broken, I could still do it, and I thought it sounded like everyone else. I also used to practice it in my village, very loudly and very often, until several people told me it was not absolutely necessary.

Spurred on by my brother, I fired that dushka until the barrel glowed hot, yelling and blasting—that was my new life. And soon I would see the remnants of the Russian convoy trying to go forward, as if they'd given up on the wounded and abandoned the burning vehicles. All of them were just revving, skidding, and swerving along the road, desperate to get out of the hellhole we'd created.

And then I saw the biggest explosion I'd ever seen. The lead Russian armored vehicle was blown into the air and the one behind it, and when they crashed to the ground, they burst into flames. That was our booby traps, and within a couple of minutes, just about every vehicle was in flames, and I could see the Russian troops fighting to get out of them.

I remember I just stood there, gaping at this scene of destruction, until, right behind me, I heard Haji Nazer Gul bellowing at me, "Keep firing! Cut them down! We want their equipment—kill them all!"

And then he patted me on the shoulder and told me I was doing great, but always to remember: "If we don't kill them, they'll kill us. Come on, kid, let's finish them."

Just then there was another huge blast from the exit end of the valley, and a rockfall came smashing down into the road, and now no one could get out, and no one ever would, not in this life.

Finally, I understood what my Islamic teachers meant by "Death to the infidel." And never again would I wonder exactly what Haji Nazer Gul meant when he said, "Gulab, they should have thought about all this before they tried to conquer us and insult the name of the Prophet and the glory of Allah."

Later that evening, when we began to pile the spoils of war onto our mountain mule carts, the air still smelled of gunpowder and death, and black smoke still wafted upward from the shattered Russian convoy.

The scene was still one of horror, but we nevertheless turned to face Mecca that evening. And there on that hillside, prostrate on our prayer mats, we thanked Allah for our great victory—*for there is no other God but Allah, and God is great.*

Looking back, that was probably the day Gulab grew up. No one could have lived through that much carnage and remained a child. He couldn't read, and he couldn't write. He knew nothing of the world beyond his mountains, and he knew little history.

But he did know the Prophet had been not only the holiest of men but also a warrior, and that he, Gulab, was already following in those hallowed footsteps. Haji Nazer Gul told him they'd all fought together that day, and that Allah stood alongside them, protecting them and helping them to victory.

Gulab believed him implicitly. He still does.

Later, however, he learned that first encounter with the enemy had not been quite so pristine perfect as he'd imagined. They had apparently wiped out two thousand Russian troops, destroyed their tanks and armored vehicles, and stolen a large amount of weaponry and ordnance.

But the men from the high villages had losses, too. Those explosions right behind Gulab had blown many of his comrades off the mountain, killed and maimed many mujahideen warriors being blasted by great hunks of rocks ripped off the mountain walls.

At the time, Gulab was, of course, unaware of how this happened.

He soon found out, however, that this was the professional work of the Russians, who, if they could climb out of their tanks and vehicles, went quickly into action with their RPG-7's, launching rocket-propelled grenades.

These are fired from portable shoulder-launchers, which weigh about fifteen pounds and can hurl a powerful grenade a thousand yards and make one hell of a bang when they hit home. The true purpose was always as an antitank missile, but the Soviets found it was just as good at splitting Afghan rocks and causing havoc among their mujahideen enemy.

That's what did the damage in the first battle. The launcher is reloadable, and an enemy using it against you must be stopped—thus Haji's yell to keep firing no matter what.

The RPG-7, with its telescopic sight, fires at a high standard, and its missiles are often heat-seeking, some of them fitted with infrared sights. It works with a gunpowder booster charge, and when the missile leaves that hot steel tube, it's clocking 350 feet per second, stabilized by two sets of fins. You have to be quick to see it coming. Two additional qualities made it vital to the mujahideen: it was relatively simple to use, and it could take out tanks.

Gulab remembers that when they swooped down to grab the remaining hardware from the defeated Russians, those launchers were top priority.

With the Russian war seriously under way, and throughout the following years, the youth of Sabray would be called to the front line every two or three weeks.

This location was never disclosed, and they all kept walking, destination unknown. It took three or four days, crossing the mountains through these ancient fighting grounds, until they reached the valley to which the Soviets were heading.

Even on the walk, the Sabray cadets were an armed military force. And they were careful not to leave tracks or disturb the ground. No Russian spy could track like they could, and they stuck to the old tribal standards, moving through the shifting shale on the hillsides and sticking to areas where they could swiftly find cover on the heavily forested slopes.

Their escape routes were always upward, because once they reached the higher slopes where the rocks were huge and tightly packed, no enemy could locate them. And if anyone tried, he would die.

By the time the mujahideen battalions arrived for an ambush, they had usually been joined by other small mountain armies, and commanders were already prepared for the forthcoming theater of war.

While media reports often suggested that the native Afghani army was disorganized, undisciplined, and mostly a bit lucky, the opposite was true. The Afghanis were brilliantly organized, with excellent intelligence, and efficient commanders, especially Gulab's older brother.

When any Russian convoy moved toward an ambush valley, it was already in enormous trouble. The mujahideen explosive was placed meticulously, snipers settled into perfect firing positions, heavy machine guns in the most destructive possible formations, swiveled to face the oncoming tanks and armored vehicles.

"I learned to select my target early," Gulab says, "and to follow it through the machine gun sights until the order came to open fire. I rarely missed, and I knew how to hit a tank crew, keeping my gun sights trained on the top part of the turret. If we don't kill them, they'll kill us."

Gulab is, in many ways, a wise historian about his own nation. He accepts that Afghanistan is a land of misconceptions and that the world has never figured out how it remained unconquered for all those hundreds of years. This didn't happen by some kind of a fluke. Mujahideen tribesmen, to this day, remain masters of guerilla warfare and masters of ambush.

They may have few sophisticated weapons, and may be too poor to buy them. But they know how to get them. They know how to engage and defeat enemies. And once they seize an advantage, they know how to finish them.

"Above all," says Gulab, "my mountains breed warriors. And these are not tribesmen as popularly conceived in Africa, an uncontrolled rabble, shouting and jumping and firing their weapons in the air, butchering women and children. Our tribesmen are born to military combat. And we breed superb commanders, tacticians, and strategists; they are men who comprehend mountain contours. Our leaders do not even need maps because of their mastery of the moon and the stars, and the great shadows of the sun. It's our enemies who need maps and charts. Up against us, they are facing the ultimate warriors: men of valor, who are born for battle. And who are unafraid to die.

"I grew up watching our field commanders in action. And in later years, I learned of great generals from other lands. I've always had one thought, however: that a top Afghani battle commander could equally direct troops from any other nation."

Nonetheless, the misconceptions remain that the mujahideen defeat their enemies simply because of the terrain. Gulab admits the mountains help them, but you don't win wars because of narrow roads.

The terrain of Afghanistan is another misconception. Beyond those dusty borders, people envision a barren land, a kind of land-locked moonscape covered in dust, sand, and boulders amid towering rock faces; and perhaps a few flat places at high altitude, suitable only for growing drugs.

That could scarcely be less accurate. The glacial history of Afghanistan is a story of great walls of ice, sometimes a thousand feet high, cleaving through the mountains, grinding up the terrain, and leaving behind a cover of fine silt. It is called khaki, and that's its color. It blows all over the place, forming a large part of the soil. It makes Afghan soil extremely fertile, rich growing earth.

There is good rainfall in many parts of the Hindu Kush, and mountain rivers rushing past are usually full of snowmelt from the high peaks of the western Himalayas. Afghani farmers need only to add water to that silt-laden earth, and they can grow melons with full orchards of fruits and nuts. They also grow large crops of potatoes, squash, tomatoes, eggplants, and peppers, as well as wheat, barley, cotton, flax, rice, and sesame.

Visitors to Afghanistan often run into either searing summer heat or blasting winter cold. They are apt to look at the dusty plains, barren mountain slopes, and deep caves and wonder where people once lived. This might give the impression of a land where life is only borderline possible; where the population is essentially Stone Age in outlook and achievement. But this is not so.

The culture of Afghanistan stretches back more than two thousand years, and it's always been a land of poetry, philosophy, and art. The world's first oil painting was discovered in Afghanistan, and the wisdom of ancient proverbs rivals those of Confucius, or a Zen koan, or Mark Twain.

Afghanistan's traditional religious beliefs have remained unaltered. That is not a misconception.

They follow Islamic traditions, and right across the nation, they celebrate the same holidays. They dress the same, eat the same food, enjoy the same music. Most of the country is multilingual, except for mountain warriors like Gulab. And all of them fear Allah and try to obey the words of the Prophet. In the northeastern mountain range, the men fear *only Allah*. No one else.

Gulab took part in many of the crushing defeats the mujahideen inflicted on the Russian armies in the terrain around Sabray. His small size may have contributed to the fact that he was never hit or even wounded throughout the campaign.

He was never moved from his position of master gunner, and where that dushka went, so went Gulab, trusted by the commanders to strip it down, clean and oil it, and then put it back together. He was subjected to inspection, like all gunnery personnel, but he swiftly learned to do the job properly.

Much of the mujahideen weaponry, especially the rockets, was provided by their friends, the Americans and the British. Everyone preferred their battle equipment, and the Afghan commanders were grateful for it. From the United States, they also received guns, money, data on battle locations, and tactical instructions. To their modern allies, it seemed that a mujahideen victory was paramount.

Sometimes US fighter jets overflew the mountains, and the population would always hear them coming. American pilots reported local people shouting and waving at their great benefactors, high in the sky, all the way from the other side of the world. Gulab now knows that there were US air bases all over the place, and they flew in from Pakistan, Iran, and Turkey. But it didn't really matter where they came from. The fact that they were there, helping Afghanistan, was all that mattered.

In the Hindu Kush, no one knew anything of the Cold War and nothing of the Soviet construction of the Wall across the middle of Berlin in 1961. Gulab had never heard of the Iron Curtain, and never caught anything on any news broadcast when the Americans told the Soviets to "tear down this wall." When President Ronald Reagan described the Soviet Union as an "evil empire," Gulab and his fellow mujahideen did hear about it eventually and came to think of him as an all-powerful friend and ally in their fight against the marauding Red Army.

No one, however, had any idea how deftly the USA would seize the chance to hit the Russians through the mujahideen in Afghanistan. They provided the sledgehammer, and the mountain men swung it. Remote as they were, it was a real comfort to know that the Americans were their friends.

Certainly the first American president involved in that war, Jimmy Carter, made his outrage clear. Immediately after the Russians attacked, he gave the Soviets exactly one month to get out of Afghanistan, or else the US would boycott the 1980 Summer Olympic Games in Moscow. Brezhnev refused, and sixty-four other nations joined the USA and refused to participate in those Games. But, boycott or no boycott, the war proceeded for Gulab under the guidance of his brother and his fellow commanders, all of whom were wounded, some killed. By the time he was twelve, he was, by any standards, a veteran.

The Afghanis kept that Soviet army bottled up inside its bases, attacking whenever possible. It was not easy, because they were hit with air strikes that destroyed mujahideen bases. There were many, many civilian casualties. And it was a time of great sadness in those mountains. But no one even considered giving up the fight.

The women of the villages were proud of their fighting men, husbands, sons, and other relatives. Indeed, if any man decided not to join the mujahideen in their holy struggle, women would ask, "What's wrong with you? Why do you not go to war?"

At the age of fourteen, it was decided that Gulab should get married, since the six-year veteran master gunner no longer felt comfortable attending school with children and helping around the house when he came home from combat.

His marriage was arranged by the family, and they chose for him a very beautiful young girl from the nearby village of Suriak. Both families knew and trusted each other, and in Islamic rural culture, that matters. They do not leave matters of such importance to the whims and excitements of the young.

"When I first saw her, I was very happy," recalls Gulab. "At our first meeting, she shone like a bright light for me, and she still does. Down all the years, I have remained delighted with her, and we have ten children: six boys and four daughters. Our oldest son is Gul Mohammed, named after my brother.

"He's been a young warrior for many years now. And he was, like me, entrusted with the family Kalashnikov since the age of twelve. If I was ever asked again to lead troops in holy combat, I would immediately make him my second in command. I trust Gul Mohammed with my heart, and he's ready to accept the highest responsibility.

"I've been teaching him all of his life, as I myself was taught. In those years between 1981 and '89, I became a hardened regular soldier. I was still only fifteen or sixteen when the Russians finally pulled out. I had seen some terrible things, but they no longer seemed so.

"War had been my life, and since I had the experience, I was generally regarded as a junior field commander. My book learning was so little, but book learning only takes you partway. You need men who have done it before. Men who have seen mistakes made by others and will not allow them to happen again.

"That was me. And my opinion was often sought and listened to, despite my youth. Anyway, I did not feel much like a youth; more like Genghis Khan. The joy of conquest had risen up within me."

Before Gulab reached his approximated fifteenth birthday, the mujahideen army knew that it was winning. The Russian troops and the Afghan government forces who marched with them already recognized the trouble they were in whenever the mountain warriors came raging into battle.

Gulab recalls a hesitation among the Russian soldiers before they began to disembark from their vehicles. The young gunner could see there was a mood of defeat among them, and it was obvious for many months that the Russian army simply could not stay there being systematically wiped out. And it was equally obvious that nothing it inflicted on the tribesmen had the slightest effect in terms of their willingness to fight on.

One such moment occurred right down on the road along the river that Gulab was defending after a Russian convoy had been decimated. Suddenly the Russians were no longer firing back. They were just working in teams, unloading their vehicles and tanks, chains of troops passing out packing cases.

At first, Gulab's commanders thought they might contain big bombs or rockets, and were considering ways to blow them right now. But then they realized the enemy was unloading weaponry, ordnance, crates of Kalashnikovs, ammunition, and RPG-7s—and throwing them into the river.

Then it dawned on them that the Russians were scared to death that if they tried to run from the battlefield, the mujahideen would most certainly shoot them down and take everything they had left behind. They must have understood now that the mujahideen army was armed with weaponry stolen from them in the first place—the spoils of victory. They were getting killed with their own guns and rockets.

The Pashtun people had once, long ago, burned their homes and contents and fled before the onslaught of Alexander the Great. Now the Russians were doing the same thing—denying military material to their enemy.

Every junior warrior in Sabray had been taught that the British general Elphinstone must have been spectacularly stupid, and that now, 140 years later, the Russians were not much better. The Soviets were endlessly clumsy and dedicated to close air support, which invariably killed many, many civilians. Which, in turn, made the entire Afghan population hate them unreservedly.

Whenever Gulab's legions hit them, the Russians switched instantly to massive-scale operations, utilizing up to fifteen thousand troops and hundreds of aircraft—the doctrines, techniques, and operational procedures of a European or Chinese theater of war.

Much worse, they underestimated totally the resolve of the Pashtun people, and very quickly the Soviet's enemy was not just a well-trained and elusive band of mujahideen warriors but an entire nation.

And the Russians could not even achieve surprise. Every time they moved, they left a gigantic footprint as they mobilized thousands of troops and hundreds of tanks and armored vehicles. It was all very predictable, and the mujahideens' intelligence network caused word to flash from village to village, across the high pastures and into the mountain garrisons: "Russian military formations on the move."

Tactically rigid and amazingly slow, the army from the north was absolutely vulnerable to the mujahideens' brand of warfare.

Gulab was taught that the Russian army advanced to Germany's Rhine River at about twenty-five miles a day during World War II. He now confirms:

I know for a fact they made only two miles per day up the Kunar Valleys in 1985. And this doggedly slow advance meant they rarely caught even a sight of us. They usually had massive firepower, and nothing much to aim it at.

We, of course, knew precisely where they were at all times, as did anyone else within a hundred-mile range. Praise Allah, they made a noise. And the mujahideen guerillas were always waiting. Our silent, skilled tribesmen plagued them from the beginning of that war to the end.

By 1986, we had some very fine modern gear, the most important of which was the FIM-92 Stinger, a portable infrared homing surface-to-air missile. It was provided by the CIA, after a historic political decision by our friend President Reagan.

The Stinger weighed thirty-four pounds loaded. It was hand-held, and it changed the course of the war—the last straw for a Soviet army which had already taken a severe battering from us. Our best estimates claim we fired 340 missiles in Kunar Province and knocked down 269 Soviet aircraft, most of them helicopters.

We've since been told that was the first time America had provided weapons for someone else to hit a Soviet army. I helped with the tactical training of our missile men: showed them how that FIM-92 could lock on and then collide with an incoming Russian Hind helicopter gunship head-on and destroy it.

To this point in missile warfare, heat seekers like the Stinger had always needed to get astern of an airborne target and blast into the hot tail exhausts. Not anymore. We just had to fire it late, at a three-mile range, incoming.

It carried a seven-pound penetrating hit-to-kill warhead with an impact fuse. Once launched, the missile quickly accelerated to more than sixteen hundred miles per hour—over twice the speed of sound. It did not take us long to realize that when this thing smashed head-on into an enemy gunship, that ended the discussion. The Russians found that out, too.

And it really upset them. Because before the arrival of the Stinger, that incoming Russian Mi-24 Hind gunship forced us to take cover. It was a "flying tank," with armored fuselage, eighty-millimeter S-8 rockets, mounted machine guns, and thousand-pound iron bombs, and it made world-record speed over the ground at more than 220 miles per hour.

But the Stinger changed everything, and we were no longer scared. We could knock that Hind out of the sky at will. Before that

US missile arrived, we hardly ever won a set-piece confrontation with the Soviets. After it arrived, we never lost one.

The mujahideen retained a treasured record of the day when the world changed: September 25, 1986, when a tribesman, an engineer named Ghaffar, fired the first Stinger at a Hind gunship and knocked it clean out of the sky near Jalalabad.

They gathered up that first Stinger tube and made a crate for it, which was sent to the US Embassy in Kabul. It was addressed to Congressman Charlie Wilson, the ex–US Navy gunnery officer from Texas who almost single-handedly persuaded the US government to get behind the mujahideen in the fight to expel the marauding Russians.

Charlie Wilson was probably the best friend from the West they ever had. He talked the CIA into providing the mountain men with those Stingers, and they rewarded him with victory over the Soviet Union. It was the most successful foreign operation the CIA ever had.

The Texas congressman believed in the Afghani cause. He had hundreds of tons of military ordnance shipped to them. And that Stinger launch tube hung on the wall of his office until his death in 2010. Without him, the task of the tribesmen would have been much, much more difficult.

Gulab is aware there are some who claim the Stingers made little impact. "But," he says, "that is absurd. They changed the world. And I speak from a rarified observation point, on the inside, on the mountainside, hunkered down against the blast of the flying rubble and shrapnel, praying for Allah to protect me.

"The mere knowledge that we owned a weapon which could blow the gunships to smithereens completely altered our mind-set. It gave us renewed hope, renewed courage, and renewed faith.

"At last we could fight a modern war, backed by this wonderful man from East Texas. Little did I know, as a teenager at the time, I would one day meet another man from there, a fellow warrior who lived about twenty-five miles from Charlie Wilson's home.

"After 1987, the war intensified, and we fought battle after battle, killing many Russians. But we suffered far fewer casualties ourselves, because their gunships never made it close enough to pound our mountain strongholds.

"The Soviets were losing two thousand troops at a time in regular battle against our two hundred. Their aerial bombardment was falling short, and thanks to Charlie Wilson, we now had sophisticated radar to spot those flying tanks in time and to obliterate them."

The Russians had had enough. With aircraft wrecks littering the mountains, they announced they were pulling out. This was cause for some elation in the villages, but the mujahideen did not trust the Kabul government. It had told the Afghan people lie after lie about the need for Communist troop support, and the mountain warriors did not believe in this Russian surrender.

The mujahideen high command ordered its battalions to keep fighting until the last Russian troops had returned from whence they came. Even when the invaders were in retreat, preparing to get out, the mujahideen hit them over and over to remind the Soviets precisely what they were dealing with—and also as a reminder that they should think very carefully before attacking a mujahideen army ever again.

Victory over the Russians was a great moment of glory for the Pashtuns. When the dust cleared, the tribesmen of the Hindu Kush were still standing tall, having confirmed yet again that no one conquers Afghanistan. *Allah is great, and may He bestow His blessings upon Charlie Wilson.*

For Gulab, it was a hard road to becoming an adult. He had to do everything very early in life, but looking back, he thinks it was probably worth it. And he recalls his pride when his elder brother first handed him command of his troops. Haji Nazer Gul was wounded at the time, and he made it clear that for the following weeks, Gulab's commands were his. At fifteen, Gulab was bigger now, and vastly experienced, and Gul's words gave him high respect.

Up there on those mountains, helping with troop formations, he'd become a real warrior; a battlefield commander. No one knew much more about it than Gulab did, because, in truth, he knew little else. Just war. Gulab's nickname in the village was already the Lion.

There were several mujahideen commanders who rejoiced in this honor. But there was no greater form of military recognition. The lion is the national symbol of Afghanistan, and has been for centuries. The first postage stamps ever issued there in 1871 (1288 on the Islamic solar calendar) were known as the lion stamps. No human image appeared on the stamps until 1937.

There was an enormous amount of work to do after the Russians left, not just "house cleaning," but also gathering up the vast array of weaponry and matériel left behind by the retreating Soviet forces. The mountain commanders utilized everything they could claim, particularly remaining transports, armored vehicles, regular vehicles, and the occasional tank, as well as rockets, grenades, ammunition clips, rifles, heavy machine guns, and launchers, not to mention bombs and land mines. They acquired only a small percentage of the prize, but it was sufficient to equip mujahideen armies long into the future.

They still had their superior ground-to-air missile gear, and that was always kept in a state of instant readiness, since no one ever knew when the nation would come under attack again. However, the bulk of the spoils of war went to the defeated Afghan government forces, and, in a way, this was partly the mujahideens' fault.

Because those mountain warriors did not fight the war for gain. They fought it for religious principle, to drive out the infidels who had defiled Islam. Thus, when the Soviets gave up, Pashtuns considered their task done, and they returned in peace to their villages. For them, it was always a Pashtun holy war, jihad, and they were ill-prepared for a voracious grab-what-you-can ending.

Equally, the Afghan government army, which fought against them behind the Russians, was absolutely ready to claim the Soviet weapons, and it knew that the owners were on the way out long before the tribesmen from the hills did. The army also knew the storage locations of the matériel, and it had access. So when the surrender whistle blew, they came in like a pack of jackals, into the 184 abandoned Soviet garrisons, seizing thousands of tons of military reserves, ammunition, food, and fuel. Gulab reflects:

When the last Soviet troops left, I was an eight-year veteran of many battles, many victories, and witness to a total of twelve hundred dead Pashtuns. I was a master machine gunner by trade, aged sixteen years—I think.

As a field commander, my opinion was sought but not always listened to during the reconfiguring of our future arsenal. We would never trust our most valuable assets in identifiable military or civilian buildings, and instead we opted for our network of high caves and underground mountain passages. These secret granite warehouses and command rooms had served us well for centuries.

The route to these was always upward and always impossible for vehicles. We thus did much heavy lifting, hauling the weaponry up to the heights using timber-hauling gear. We took everything into places where no foreign invaders would ever find them.

Our needs were not so great as the government army's, which planned to patrol the entire country. And they received three thousand trucks from the Russians, which would always be largely useless in our part of the world. Our own victorious army would quietly fade out of sight until the next would-be conqueror ventured into our mountainous territory.

I do remember those final days of the Soviet occupation, and even I could tell, as a teenager, there was confusion among the village elders. The Russian withdrawal from Afghanistan was negotiated by a Kabul government whose forces had been defeated by the mujahideen. My commanders found this very strange, since our military policy was to fight and kill the infidels until they were gone. And whether or not Kabul had some kind of agreement with Moscow, the infidel was still here. That we understood.

Our continuing strategy remained unaltered. We would hit them whenever and wherever we saw fit. We would not recognize the Afghan government's agreement to allow them safe passage out of the country. The warrior tribes of Kabul answer only to Allah.

I have no doubt that others will point out that Russia's exit from my country was a masterpiece of military strategy: that they were not really defeated, and left in a coordinated, deliberate, and professional manner, while leaving behind a functioning government and a stronger military.

But that's only a point of view. They left because they could not stay, because in the end, we would have wiped them out—all of them. By 1988, they were confined to city garrisons, and they dared not set foot in the mountain ranges of the northeast.

I suppose they left in some kind of order, but it should not be forgotten that they lost over five hundred more men on that retreat, all of them under mujahideen attack, and almost all of them in the steep passes of Kunar Province.

The Soviet retreat began in May 1988, with fifty thousand troops taking the same two northern routes out as the ones they'd used to come in. The western road was from Kandahar, in the far south, up through Farah Rud and Herat to the Turkmenistan border town of Kushka. The eastern one began in Ghazni, Gardez, and Jalalabad, and on to Kabul, where the main road swung north, up past Bagram and into the mountains.

This was the dangerous part, where the mujahideen waited all along the road to the border and the Friendship Bridge connecting Afghanistan and Uzbekistan, over the Amu Dar'ya River. The first phase went reasonably well for both sides, but the second phase of the withdrawal, which took place along the eastern corridor in the dead of winter between January 2 and February 15, 1989, was difficult for everyone.

The bulk of the Soviet Fortieth Army, thirty thousand men, traveled through ice, snow, and fog to reach the bridge. Their armored vehicles held up, with hundreds of them deployed into a steel corridor designed to keep the mujahideen at bay.

In those final days, the men from the mountains killed the last forty enemy troops of this war, firing, as ever, from the high escarpments, while watching those lines and lines of armored Soviet BTR-80 armored personnel carriers rumbling north, bound for their old military headquarters in Termez.

Gulab never saw them cross the bridge, but his commanders positioned unseen observers to record the historic victory: photographing from afar the men of the great northern superpower, who had fought and lost.

The last commander of the mighty Soviet Fortieth Army, the long-serving Colonel General Boris Gromov, finally marched out of Afghanistan, north across the bridge, alone, behind his defeated men. The general was a holder of the Gold Star Medal, and a Hero of the Soviet Union.

"I am told," says Gulab, "the general bore his humiliation bravely."

Back in the villages, they realized slowly that there was a new regime governing the Soviet Union. Listening to their little radios, sometimes connecting to the BBC World Service, the tribesmen finally learned how traumatic the 1980s had been for the Soviets.

Leonid Brezhnev, the veteran leader they blamed for the invasion of Afghanistan, died in 1982. His successor, Yuri Andropov, died two years later. Konstantin Chernenko lasted only thirteen months and died in 1985, and the doyen of foreign ministers, Andrei Gromyko, was leader of the Supreme Soviet for only three years. He retired in 1988, and died the following year, within weeks of his defeated army leaving Afghanistan.

The new man was Mikhail Gorbachev, and he seemed far less unpredictable than the rest of them. The Pashtuns' friend President Reagan seemed to like him, and the new American president, George H. W. Bush, was working with him when the Berlin Wall came down in November 1989.

Russia seemed to be a less threatening place now, and the mujahideen came to believe they had a lot to do with that. Mr. Gorbachev taught his people to concentrate on trade and prosperity rather than on warfare. No one really knew how much they were affected by the damage the tribal army had inflicted on them.

"We showed," says Gulab, "that a skilled, determined army can bring down the armed forces of a superpower. If we'd been given even half of the modern equipment the Soviets possessed, we would have beaten them in a couple of years. They weren't bad fighters, but they were nothing like as good as we were.

"They lasted so long because they were ten times better equipped than us. When President Reagan and Charlie Wilson provided the Stinger missile and we could at last attack their air power—well, the game was over for the Soviets. Military superiority does not guarantee victory.

"We, in turn, discovered once more that triumph over adversity is better than succumbing to it."

- 2 -

A LAND OF DEFIANT MEN

While Gulab can neither read nor write, he grew into a man while fighting the Russians. He still says, "People are sometimes surprised at my lack of formal education, but I always tell them the same thing: I never had time for education. I was too busy fighting."

However, he is adamant that his people are not uneducated tribal killers. And they have a long history of learning. So far as Gulab knows, every last warrior who fights jihad with the mujahideen obeys the teachings of the Prophet Muhammad. And that includes the part that forbids the murder of innocent people and even prisoners of war. The tribesmen regard themselves as holy warriors, and claim to understand perfectly what is right and what is wrong.

"I know very well there are rabid Muslim sects who obey no one's teaching and act in defiance of the will of Allah," he says. "But they do not represent the people of Afghanistan, nor do they represent Islamic teaching. They defile the word of the Prophet, and they do not fight jihad, whatever they claim. True holy warriors despise all terrorists as cheap murderers."

And alongside Gulab's warrior training, there was also plenty of religious study and instruction. Sabray's holy studies, which took place after regular lessons, were never compromised. Every day, he would sit cross-legged on the ground with other junior soldiers outside the village mosque learning the creeds of the Koran in more and more depth.

They were taught six *kalimas,* which were compiled especially for children to memorize and thus understand the fundamentals of Muslim beliefs, based upon the narration of the Prophet (as Gulab always adds, "Peace be upon him").

Between fighting battles in the mountains, Gulab learned the first *kalima,* the *tayyabah,* or the words of purity: *La ilaha ill Allah Muhammadur—Rasul Allah.*

In long hours of study, he learned the words of testimony, that no one but Allah is worthy of worship. He learned the word for glorification, *tumjeed,* glory and praise to Allah. And he learned the word for unity (*tauhid*).

The fifth *kalima* taught him the word for penitence (*astaghfar*), and how for every sin, known and unknown, he must seek forgiveness from Allah, *the Most High and Most Great.*

The sixth *kalima* taught every child to reject disbelief, *since there is none worthy of worship, save for Allah.*

Holy lessons began and ended with a prayer, and as the months and years wore on, and Gulab witnessed even more death in battle at close quarters, the presence of Allah in his life took on a stark but comforting meaning. He understood that he was required to live by the compassionate words of the Prophet, even though at that age he was not exactly sure what that meant; especially since he was also required to open fire on Russian enemies with a heavy machine gun.

Education is very important in the villages of the Hindu Kush. Not Western education, but an awareness of their deep culture going back thousands of years. Gulab's father, Azer Alam, was a learned man, and so was his grandfather. Gulab's earliest memories are of his father, a respected village elder, teaching holy studies to all the children, Gulab included, and also to the adults.

Azer Alam held a unique position in the community, being by far the most educated man and subsequently the most powerful. No one in Sabray would move very far without consulting him. His station was superior to the mullah, the local cleric, because of his advanced learning, and all of the teaching classes revolved around his knowledge.

He conducted his classes outside, on a daily basis: one hour for mathematics, another hour for English, and then on to the teachings of the Prophet Muhammad. Boys' classes were, of course, separate from the girls', and the religion of Islam was never very far away from the students. From the earliest ages, the young people saw the older men and women at prayer in the village mosque five times a day. They understood, above all else, there was no life beyond the Prophet.

By the time the children reached the ages of six or seven, they were learning the first *kalima,* which is the irrefutable pillar of Islam: *There is no God but Allah.* They all understood that, and it's the bedrock of all Islamic teaching, their faith, and their devotion to God.

Every member of the mujahideen is devout in his belief in the laws of Islam. He is fighting jihad, the most powerful force in life. That is perhaps why they all understand and accept that Afghanistan can never be conquered.

No one has ever subjugated that country, and very probably no one ever will. Because they do not accept defeat.

"We will never surrender," Gulab has said of his people, "and even if we did, for reasons of convenience, no one—repeat, no one— would ever mean it, nor believe it.

"We all understand that every man, woman, and child must, if necessary, answer a call to arms. And we were brought up to accept that; to realize that one day we may all be required to face our enemy, to stand tall and fight to the death, until there is not one of us left standing.

"In our homeland, our tribal enemies understand that, and to make war on a place like Sabray is likely to result in very tragic consequences. The Al Qaeda armies may come to my village, sometimes to request supplies, sometimes to ask for shelter or water, and sometimes they attempt to bully our people, or even recruit them.

"But I can tell you one thing: those swaggering tribal combatants think very carefully before opening fire in Sabray, despite that noisy, boastful way they have about them."

A few decades ago, the Hindu Kush was far more lawless. Indeed, Gulab's own father was murdered, shot down by a Taliban raiding party. Gulab was only five at the time, but he saw it and recalls it all vividly. His mother never really got over it.

Everyone understood the killing was political; that the immense authority Gulab's father wielded in the local communities made him too influential. Quarrels over land, buildings, crops, and business seethed throughout the villages.

In Sabray, it was very nearly impossible to pass any law or make any tribal contract without Azer Alam's permission. His words were that powerful. The murder was long ago now, but for Gulab and his brothers, it is always present. Hurt, anguished, and furious, they held a meeting and agreed about the precise identity of the killer who had cut down the head of the family.

And right there, an ancient tribal rage rose up among them, with the curved blade of revenge settling in their midst. And years went by, during which time they never took their eyes off their father's murderer. It was an unspoken plan that nothing would happen until Gulab reached warrior status, on his twelfth birthday.

By then, he was in the chain of command among the battle ranks of the mujahideen. He was a blooded infantryman, sworn to defeat the Russians, who were blundering through his land in their tanks and armored vehicles.

Gulab remembers well the night it was decided the deed must be done—that their father's murder must now be avenged. And while tribal etiquette still forbids elaboration, the brothers decided that the murderer would be cut down with a two-handed tribal sword rather than a modern carbine bullet.

The sword was removed from its sacred place and taken by Azer Alam's warrior sons and their armed family supporters to the man's home. And there, in a Pashtun tradition that goes back millenniums, it was swung in a swift and savage arc.

No one will ever disclose who actually swung the blade and completed this ancient circle of revenge. But it was carried out under the merciless Pashtun laws that have held the tribes together for thousands of years. "We occasionally forgive," says Gulab, "but we never forget.

"Sometimes we all made the short journey to Asadabad, to the principal mosque, where Imams of high learning sometimes gathered. My own father had gone there occasionally, but we mostly stuck to our own mosque, built in the center of the village and readily identifiable as a place of serious worship.

"It stood on two floors with glass windows. The top section was for summer; the lower part for winter. Its doors were always open during daylight, and inside was an enormous oriental rug on which we knelt to praise Allah and ask for guidance and mercy, and offer our thanks for the resounding victory over the Soviets. We do talk to Allah, but he does not reply to us directly.

"A local Islamic mosque is a community center open and ever welcoming for every man to enter and listen to the sacred words of the Imam. And there, as often as necessary, we would renew and confirm our faith, always stating our unshakeable belief that there is no other God but Allah and that no other deserves our worship.

"I was always watching for one of our children to display an extra depth in his learning, both academic and religious, perhaps following in the footsteps of his grandfather, and with a destiny to become a learned man. But the older boys were more interested in the warrior class of Sabray, in the footsteps of their father, not grandfather. And I was proud of their youthful bravery and their certainty of our ways.

"This was one of the few times in my life when I was not absolutely preoccupied with the demands of war. But we all listened in to the radio and to the endless buzz of the tribesmen with their stories and knowledge from across the mountains."

Gulab's family business was timber, cleaving down trees that were often a thousand years old. It was a hard but very profitable way to make a living, and when he returned from the fighting, he set about making as much money as possible.

For mujahideen warriors, the months leading up to the dissolution of the Soviet Union on December 26, 1991, were the harbingers of a peaceful decade in the mountains of the Hindu Kush. They were the rightful spoils of a bloody struggle. Gulab spent his time working among the trees, many of which were harder than granite.

"They were a colossal weight," he says, "but valuable. And with my young family growing fast, I seemed to need money more than ever before. I insured that everyone went to school and that the older children prayed with the elders in the village mosque."

Of course, there was no machinery. Those massive trees had to be taken down and then cut sufficiently small to be loaded onto mule carts, or in some cases horse-drawn wagons. They also had to find a way to drag the timber down to the road for loading. Wood is heavy stuff, and the work was very hard, especially hauling it down the steep slopes and through the forested lower areas.

But Gulab's family had done this for many generations, and once a big tree is down, there is a ready market waiting in Pakistan for hardwood from the mountain forests. It is a well-organized industry, with timber merchants from across the border patrolling the main road below the Sabray escarpments, watching for the tree trunks to be hauled down.

Gulab was determined to excel and become a village leader. And he understood that the more work he did, the better his prospects. So he worked all hours and built up his savings. But there were those who resented his growing fortune, as he cut the timber from the family lands and prospered in a private and legal way. No one said anything, though, because Gulab's reputation as a fighting mujahideen commander was already established. The truth is, no one would have dared to either attack or criticize his family—not with Haji Nazer Gul and the young Lion standing as leaders. Also, they remembered what had befallen the man who murdered their father.

"They are all we know," says Gulab of his village's tribal laws. "And it seems strange to us that everything in the West has to be written down, even a man's birth date.

"We have a different way of looking at things and conducting our lives, because we obey a set of Pashtun laws that have been handed down from generation to generation over thousands of years. There are, however, only ten of them. And they have, down the centuries, kept us on a straight and narrow path; guidance approved by both Allah and the Prophet Muhammad, peace be upon him."

The window of relative peace in the mountains came to end with news of a new threat from within that did not necessarily follow the same Pashtun laws that Gulab's village did.

"We heard of the resignation of Mr. Gorbachev, of the possible illness of President Reagan, but above all this, we heard the rumors and the reports of the rise of a new force in our part of the world: the Taliban, the fundamentalists of Islam. Most of the news was coming from across the border in Pakistan, where this strict interpretation of the Koran was being welded into a political party by the fanatical 'spiritual leader,' Mohammed Omar, a Pashtun by birth."

Mullah Omar, a former Islamic religious teacher from Kandahar, was a tall, one-eyed cleric who had been wounded while fighting in the front line against the Russians in 1987. Gulab had not met him personally, but he was, from all accounts, an excellent marksman, a formidable character, and, apparently, already the closest friend of an obscure Sunni cleric named Osama bin Laden, whose rise to power was not yet well known.

Omar and bin Laden both lived in the borderlands between Afghanistan and northern Pakistan, not far from Gulab's village. Mullah Omar named himself, very early on, "commander of the faithful."

Gulab says wryly that he has no information on whether Allah approved this or not. "I had my doubts then. Still do."

In those years, the very early 1990s, Mullah Omar's Taliban were not really instilled with the history and tradition as later reported. It claimed to enforce strict Sharia law, but there were, immediately, indications of harsh and brutal treatment of women, actions that the mountain Pashtuns very definitely did not approve of.

The mullah might have been commander of the faithful, but Gulab himself was faithful, and he was not sure whose edict suddenly placed him under the command of this new mullah.

"Did this mean I was somehow less faithful?" he wondered. "None of us in the high villages were sure about all this. And anyway, at first it was all rumor. No facts. Nothing official."

Indeed, the new Taliban started from very small beginnings, consisting mostly of students from Islamic schools in Pakistan. These had been built for Afghani refugees from strife-torn areas where citizens had been caught in the endless battles between government forces and a succession of warlords.

Kabul was often under siege, but it was peaceful in the Sabray area as well as in most of the North. Many people had fled the country during the Russian war, and now it seemed that there were a few hundred students on the Pakistan border who had rushed to the banner of the new Taliban.

The most frequently repeated story of the rising Taliban emerged in the spring of 1994, when neighbors near Mullah Omar's now permanent home in Kandahar told him that the local governor had abducted two teenage girls, shaved their heads, and taken them to a camp, where they were raped.

Led by the mullah, thirty Taliban warriors, with only sixteen rifles among them, charged in, freed the girls, and promptly hanged the governor from the gun barrel of a tank. This brought instant fame, and quickly there were fifteen thousand more students from the madrassas of Pakistan on the march, crossing the Afghan border and heading for the mullah's new Taliban stronghold in Kandahar.

By late 1994, Mullah Omar had an army. It was badly equipped and low on munitions, but its core was Pashtun, and its warriors brought with them generations of war-fighting instincts. That year, led by the mullah, they assembled in Maiwand, a small village fifty miles west of Kandahar. Although insignificant today, Maiwand carries enormous notoriety in the annals of Afghanistan's military history.

Because here on July 27, 1880, on the plains of Kandahar Province, the Afghan armed forces, commanded by Mohammed Ayub Khan, inflicted one of the most serious defeats ever sustained by the British army in India. They lost almost a thousand men, with another two hundred wounded, from two entire brigades commanded by Brigadier General George Burrows, a decorated hero who helped put down the Indian mutiny.

Ayub Khan, his infantry blasted by British artillery, lost in excess of three thousand, but his huge force of twenty-five thousand Afghan warriors overwhelmed the British and Indian invaders, and in the end routed them. Contemporary description of the decisive assault describes the British left flank "giving way and rolling as a great wave to the right, swept away by the pressure of the Afghan attack."

To this day, the Battle of Maiwand stands infamous in British history—still referred to, colloquially, as "My God! Maiwand." For when that left flank gave way, the Sixty-Sixth Regiment of Foot (the Berkshire Regiment) was almost wiped out. The regimental commanding officer, Lieutenant Colonel James Galbraith, led the final fifty-six of his troops into a mud-walled garden in the nearby scattering of huts at Khig. And there, on the edge of a ravine, against more than twenty thousand Pashtuns, they made their last stand.

The colonel died holding the regimental colors aloft, and with just eleven men of the Sixty-Sixth still fighting and still inflicting huge losses on their enemy, they elected to charge out of the garden and die in battle.

An elaborately framed account of this action, written by an Afghan artillery officer, hangs prominently in a London museum. It reads:

These men charged from the shelter of a garden, and died with their faces to the enemy, fighting to the death. So fierce was their charge, and so brave their actions, no Afghan dared to approach to cut them down.

So, standing in the open, back to back, firing steadily, every shot counting, surrounded by thousands, these British soldiers died. It was not until the last man was shot down that the Afghans dared to advance on them. The behavior of those last eleven was the wonder of all who saw it.

Infamous as a massacre in England and glorious as a victory in Afghanistan, the name Maiwand is commemorated in art and literature in many places, from Kabul to Reading in Berkshire, England. And there one of the largest cast-iron statues in the world, the thirty-one-foot *Maiwand Lion*, stands on a pedestal near the center of town, in tribute to the 328 local men who died in that far-flung battle in the Second Anglo-Afghan War.

Maiwand thus became a military byword, and there is none greater in the Afghan language. And in 1994, with a commendable sense of history, that was the place Commander Mullah Omar chose for his Taliban starting point on a relentless march toward power.

On that morning, he set off with his untested Taliban troops to conquer Kandahar, in the footsteps of the immortal Ayub Khan. Perched three thousand feet above sea level, this is Afghanistan's second largest city, and a major trading center for wool, cotton, and silk. Kandahar is a fertile growing area for fruit, grains, and tobacco, with two other prime distinctions: it is the spiritual capital of the Pashtun nation, and the pomegranate capital of the world.

When Mullah Omar reached the city in 1994, many Pashtun tribal leaders, warlords, and commanders surrendered almost immediately to his largely Pashtun army. For the first time in many months, a semblance of order was restored in Kandahar, where total lawlessness had reigned and a succession of atrocities had terrified the population.

The Taliban warriors grabbed border crossing points, ammunition dumps, and militia strongholds, while seizing twelve more surrounding provinces not under Afghan government control. The mullah's views were stern, but there was relief among the people for the discipline and control that he imposed.

The final area of uncontrolled Afghani warfare was in Kabul itself, 135 miles from the Sabray area. Several militia leaders were striving to take the city, fighting one another as well as the government army. The militias didn't possess the discipline and determination of Mullah Omar's veterans, and they were all defeated roundly by the well-ordered Afghani troops, led by the Islamic State's brilliant minister for defense, Ahmad Shah Massoud, a truly formidable man known locally as the Lion of Panjshir.

Massoud, a highly decorated mujahideen commander, had defeated the Red Army in Gulab's northeastern mountains *thirteen times* in the 1980s. The Soviets finally just gave up and completely stopped trying to fight Afghanistan's greatest military leader on his home territory around the village of Jangalak in the Panjshir Valley. Gulab speaks of him with immense respect:

Everyone knew of Commander Massoud. He was a government minister who had personally taken up the sword, to defend his country. Such men are rare, even in my land of quiet, devout heroes. And this man was extraordinary: a politician and an inspired military tactician; a lover of poetry, and a man of magnetic personality; a battle commander whose stature and authority seemed to surge up from the rose-brown sandy Pashtun earth upon which he stood.

The exploits of Commander Massoud have now passed into folklore; our children are taught of his ways and his strategies. They say that in the high valleys, on certain evenings, the thunder of his guns may still be heard. Twelve years after his cruel and barbaric assassination at the hands of bin Laden's suicide bombers, the Lion of Panjshir will not be silenced.

I speak of this Afghan giant not just because we fought for the same holy cause, at the same time, in similar country. But because I knew him as a neighbor, since the Panjshir Valley is situated in a range of mountains northwest of Sabray.

The residents are fellow Pashtuns and have been our good friends for generations. Like us, the men of the Panjshir have a fierce streak of independence. And when the Russians marched into our country, the men of that beautiful valley rose up as one, and, like us, declared holy war on the invading infidels.

Like us, they were prepared to fight to the death, and it was from their land of plenty, redolent with mulberry trees and other fruit orchards, that the great mujahideen commander came to us. Down the centuries, the Panjshir people had always journeyed over the mountains to Sabray and stayed with us on their way to the Pakistan border.

With the onset of war against the Soviets, they were quite frequent visitors, with many families leaving for Pakistan; merchants and dealers heading for the border for trade; even military personnel going to the border mysteriously, perhaps to receive armaments or even Pakistani cash to finance and supply our war effort.

And that was where Ahmad Shah Massoud entered our lives. He came from across those mountains, on a journey to the border, and was greeted by us in long-standing friendship. I forget the actual date, but on this night, he came at dusk and dined with the elders. But it suddenly snowed, heavily. Great blizzards howled across the Hindu Kush peaks, and when we awoke at first light, we were in a white world, and it was obvious that Commander Massoud and his bodyguards were going nowhere.

This was not a sudden, intense winter storm. This was winter, arriving with a flourish and locking us all into our village for the duration. The only way out was downward, but that was impossible for Massoud, because the Russian army at the time was encamped way below us, and while they would never have the nerve to come up and attack, neither would we have the nerve to go down and confront them face-on. Right here we had a winter standoff, and that night it snowed again.

Ahmad Shah Massoud was about to spend the dark, cold months in Sabray, where there was a lot of fuel, plenty of heat, well-stored food, and much to discuss. He did not seem in any way depressed by this and quickly joined a fellow Pashtun community with routines and practices with which he was quite familiar.

We were in the mid- to late 1980s, and I was a very young gunnery officer. Commander Massoud would sit among all of the mujahideen warriors who fought for the same cause, and endlessly discuss strategy. A master of ambush, and a ruthless tactician, he told us of great victories of the recent past and outlined even greater ones yet to come.

I remember his confidence, his certainty that Allah fought alongside us, and that He would guide us to the very end, until the Soviets left. Technically, he was a supreme exponent of war, and it was not difficult to understand he had earned an engineering degree at the University of Kabul in the 1970s.

In some ways, he spoke as an engineer, with careful talks on the angles of gunfire, the importance of machine gun placement, of skillfully laid mines and bombs, the crucial aspects of timing—not too early with our detonations, never too late.

There was no doubt he was a master, and his subjects were the only ones I had ever known. I loved talking to him, and he was always both patient and generous—a help to everyone in Sabray that winter. And before the snows had melted, he had made us better, and in the battles to come, we would be sharper than ever; more thoughtful, better planners, more strategic.

He spoke long and often with our village elders, he prayed with us constantly, and his hatred of Communism was an inspiration, occupied as we officially were by the Red Army. He also disliked the many militias that caused so much trouble and unhappiness in our country. He was avowed to rid Afghanistan of all of them: Russians, warlords, and anyone else who hindered our possibilities for peace and prosperity.

We all watched the commander marching with his men resolutely up toward the Pakistan border after the snow melted. I was sad to see him leave, and I never saw him again.

Ten years passed, to the mid-nineties, and the rise of the Taliban seemed unstoppable. Mullah Omar's troops carried most of the country before them, and the only barrier to their seizing total power was Commander Massoud, who did not approve of their fundamentalist interpretation of Islam, hated their harsh treatment of women, and believed their many versions of the Koran did not follow the true teachings of the Prophet.

In the West, his destruction of sections of the Soviet army had made him, well, lionized. The *Wall Street Journal* once described him as "The Afghan Who Won the Cold War." And now he had a new enemy, Mullah Omar's Taliban, which was rapidly joining Sheik Osama bin Laden's Al Qaeda, not to mention almost thirty thousand Pakistani troops, sent to help the mullah and the sheik get Afghanistan under control.

Thus armed and primed, the one-eyed mullah understood he needed to attack and seize the capital, Kabul, and take command of the country. In 1995 he began shelling the city and, with his troops on the march, unaccustomed to anything but victory, the Taliban stormed toward the outer ramparts.

And there they ran into a wall of fire, as the Islamic State's forces, commanded brilliantly by Ahmad Shah Massoud, cut them down in droves. The master of the ambush proceeded to inflict a devastating defeat upon the Taliban, unleashing a withering machine gun barrage, which even the Soviets had never been able to withstand.

The Taliban retreated, cut up and decimated, and with profound hatred in their hearts for the victorious Lion of Panjshir. Their losses were heavy, but they were reinforced by Pakistan, which was sending in thousands and thousands of soldiers—possibly up to thirty thousand. And these joined the fourteen thousand Afghan Taliban fighters, and three thousand of bin Laden's Al Qaeda militants, all fighting Commander Massoud.

Massoud had no wish for his army to commit suicide, nor to fight street battles in Kabul, so he retreated north to his homeland in the Hindu Kush, still avowed to fight the Taliban. His reputation was sealed as the commander in chief of the Northern Alliance.

On September 27, 1996, Mullah Omar's army entered Kabul unopposed and established the Islamic Emirate of Afghanistan. It was a regime that would be ever favorable to Pakistan, and one of its first actions was to accept an invitation from Ahmad Shah Massoud to meet in Maidan Shar, twenty-five miles southwest of Kabul, to plan a future government for Afghanistan.

The Taliban turned up but declined to cooperate. It was later learned that the Taliban leader who greeted Commander Massoud was shot dead for not taking an obvious chance to personally execute the revered government minister from the Panjshir Valley.

Massoud's acute dislike of the Taliban understandably increased. And on an almost weekly basis, he was hearing of unimaginably cruel actions by Mullah Omar's men. It was, after all, an army that had begun its reign with thousands of frenzied students hanging a provincial governor from the gun barrel of a tank. If anything, its bloodthirsty instincts grew worse, and its propensity to stone women to death for alleged adultery angered Ahmad Shah Massoud hugely.

He was still the one man in the north of the country with whom the Taliban dreaded to tangle. Commander Massoud was vociferous in his condemnation of their creeds and methods, and he was never even remotely afraid of them. He just plain did not approve of the Taliban.

One of his most famous statements was: "It is our conviction, and we believe, that both men and women were created by the Almighty. Both have equal rights. Women can pursue an education, women can pursue a career, and women can play a role in society . . . just like men."

In the end, the Taliban leadership—likely in consultation with bin Laden—accepted that there was only one way to take over Massoud's one-third of the country, and that was to get rid of him.

Bin Laden sent a team posing as journalists, with bombs hidden in their cameras, to the commander's offices in Takhar Province, way up in the north of the country on the Tajikistan border. Takhar is a big place with a thousand villages and almost a million people, and its name will live in notoriety because of what happened there on September 9, 2001.

The terrorists detonated their bombs, blasting Commander Massoud across the room. Desperate doctors and medics rushed to help, and a military helicopter came in to evacuate him to a field hospital.

Sadly, he died before he got there. Ahmad Shah Massoud was only forty-eight. Gulab says quietly, "I've always thought it was awful that the great resistance fighter should have died at the hands of cowards—men who were not even brave enough to identify themselves."

Massoud was the finest mujahideen commander of the second half of the twentieth century, a man of enormous accomplishments. Had he lived, the Americans might never have sent troops to Afghanistan. And his death brought terrible sadness to the people of Kunar and throughout the entire country.

He was the only Afghan chief who never left the country throughout the wars against the Soviets and the Taliban, and within weeks of his death, he was declared a National Hero of Afghanistan.

"I still remember those September days," says Gulab, "and the pall of sorrow which settled over our country, especially in the northern and eastern mountains. And we instantly blamed the followers of this strange war-loving Saudi cleric, Osama bin Laden, who reputedly lived high in our mountains, northeast of Sabray." He continues:

> I never went up there, but there were many rumors and stories about him; how he provided large amounts of cash to recruit and train his killers in camps which were constructed on the slopes of the giant escarpments.
>
> His Saudi nationality was unusual. There are not that many millionaire Arabs from Riyadh living in caves in the Hindu Kush, trying to persuade kids to commit suicide while blowing up his various perceived enemies. And then there was his apparent commitment

to Mullah Omar's Taliban, the joint training camps, and shared desire for an all-powerful tribal council which would rule Afghanistan.

Bin Laden was politically clueless; otherwise he would never have dreamed of assassinating Ahmad Shah Massoud, a man to whom a large part of Afghanistan was unashamedly devoted. What could he possibly hope to gain by alienating almost half the nation, in the land which was currently sheltering him from his enemies?

The workings of this mind will doubtless continue to baffle people for many years to come. And on September 10, 2001, a million questions were permeating the national sadness over the murder of the towering mujahideen commander.

Little did we know, bin Laden's presence would become even more prominent just one day later, when the Saudi killer would make world headlines.

When bin Laden's terrorists flew those planes into Manhattan's World Trade Center, we were slow to find out. In the Hindu Kush, it was nine and a half hours further on. So Sabray was in twilight when the planes hit the towers. And because we had no electricity, most villagers went to bed when it was too dark to see and awakened when the sun began to rise up over the eastern peaks of the Himalayas.

Thus it was morning when our first radios were turned on and we heard that there were almost three thousand dead. It wasn't long before we also heard that the USA was about ready to declare war on anyone who was sheltering Osama bin Laden.

And we truly had no idea what this would ultimately mean for us. Osama bin Laden had always seemed remote from us: he was backed by Pakistan and apparently fled to that country. He was most certainly not Pashtun, nor even an Afghan.

Understand, we had no television, and our radio reception was erratic. No one had the slightest idea what those two gigantic skyscrapers looked like, either when they were hit by the aircraft, or afterward, when they had both caved in.

And it was likely forgotten that our beloved martyred Commander Massoud had addressed the European Parliament five months previously in April 2001 and issued a warning. He stated that his intelligence network had "gained limited knowledge" about an imminent large-scale terrorist attack on US soil.

Massoud was a devout Muslim, and none of us approves of innocent citizens being killed. I say "none"—except for a very few who embrace a kind of lawless terrorism which is not only foreign to Pashtuns but is offensive in the extreme.

We all understood from the radio broadcasts that the USA president was absolutely furious that his nation had been attacked in this way.

But despite constant alerts that the US was preparing some terrible vengeance against someone, it never once occurred to us that our American friends and allies would be angry with us as a nation. Had not the mujahideen and the United States stood shoulder to shoulder against the Soviets in the 1980s?

But as weeks went by, the mountain Pashtuns were surprised at the number of US fighter jets flying overhead—with the main question being, why Afghanistan? There's nothing here for the United States, except this half-crazed Arab killer hiding in some of the most remote mountain strongholds.

Of course, they knew bin Laden was up there, and they'd heard about his training camps for terrorists. But the White Mountain range, where he was believed to be in hiding, was a long and arduous climb even for Pashtun mountain men, and no one particularly cared to meet this deranged foreign cleric who appeared to have started World War III.

The White Mountain range forms a natural border between Afghanistan and Pakistan. In that part of the frontier, where the Khyber Pass cuts through, the peaks are more than fifteen thousand feet above sea level, a snowbound wall that towers above the surrounding hills.

The people understood that bin Laden lived somewhere up there—according to rumors, in a deep complex of caves and tunnels. And from where they stood, it was fairly obvious the Americans agreed. For about three weeks, they saw the US warplanes streaking across the mountains above, and then on October 7, twenty-six days after the 9/11 attack, the bombing began.

They occasionally heard the US onslaught echoing back across these remote and empty mountains, but it did not sound like the end of the world. It seemed controlled and contained, and they grew used to the explosions all through the long autumn days before the snows once more buried great swathes of the land and winter arrived.

December came, and there was increasing news of President

Bush's war on terrorism. Everyone knew there were terrorists in the mountains, but it still seemed very separate from the Afghan nation. This bunch of wild men hiding in the White Mountains could not, after all, have knocked down the World Trade Center, although it did seem they were getting the blame for it.

Even Sheik bin Laden, whose photographs showed him always walking with a long stick, seemed an unlikely terrorist, though he was identified on radio as the mastermind and planner behind the attacks. Those who actually carried out the plot were plainly dead.

But in early December, the Americans began a thunderous aerial bombardment over a cave-riddled section of the White Mountains known as Tora Bora, an ancient tribal headquarters for Pashtuns at war. That was the bin Laden hideout, surrounded by several hundred of his followers.

By this time, the United States was preparing to move an army of Special Forces up there and take on Al Qaeda head-on. But first there was the bombing. In the course of the next three days, US bombers were reputed to have dropped seven hundred thousand pounds of ordnance on the mountain, with each B-52 carrying twenty five-hundred-pounders.

This was around-the-clock bombing, presumably on the basis that if you destroy every last inch of the terrain, you're bound to get the cleric. And to make doubly sure, the Americans dropped an enormous BLU-82 "Daisy Cutter," a fifteen-thousand-pound bomb that had been used in the 1991 Gulf War to clear minefields.

When that thing hit, it shuddered the mountains like an earthquake. And the United States followed it in with a new armada of B-52s dropping dozens more five-hundred-pounders. Almost all Afghan accounts confirm that bin Laden's trench had been destroyed.

No one who was anywhere near the Hindu Kush could have missed that onslaught. Gulab says it changed the landscape, altered the shape of the White Mountains, blew up entire mountaintops, and filled in crevasses and valleys. Mountain men said that certain areas were no longer recognizable.

But the chilling suspicion was that bin Laden had escaped, despite those bombs blasting percussion shocks throughout the cave and tunnels.

Hundreds had died, but there was no body and no sign of the sheik.

Every Al Qaeda prisoner swore to God he'd made it out sometime before those BLU-82s ripped the landscape asunder. And there might have been seven of them.

The United States swore to take him—dead or alive.

COULD ANYONE STILL BE ALIVE?

All through the dark winter months of December, January, and February, it was obvious that the anger of the United States could not be stilled. The tribesmen, huddled around iron stoves while snow fell constantly over the high slopes and the winds howled relentlessly through leafless trees, heard the BBC World Service announce that the Americans were not satisfied with the near-total decimation of the White Mountains and would not be satisfied until they saw the dead body of Sheik Osama bin Laden.

The only sound that awakened the silent winter hillsides of the Hindu Kush was the shattering scream of US fighter aircraft racing overhead, still heading up to Tora Bora and the high passes through which Osama and his henchmen had almost certainly fled.

And yet, throughout all of this overhead mayhem, America seemed not to wish the local people any harm. No pilot ever dropped a bomb on them or anyone who lived anywhere near. There was no strafing, no instructions, no demands, no communiqués.

The US military was just conducting its regular business in pursuit of this foreigner who had, with no invitation, parked himself and his followers in one of the most secret Pashtun strongholds, up on the highest border with Pakistan.

Almost five months after 9/11, no evidence whatsoever had linked the terrorist attacks with the tribes from the northeast. The United States had literally flung the Taliban out of office in November when they retook Kabul, with their own forces fighting alongside the late Commander Massoud's Northern Alliance, plus a coalition of British and Canadian forces.

There was a new American-backed government in Kabul. But the mood remained hostile, as US forces kept after bin Laden—on one famous occasion, angrily threatening "to bomb Pakistan back to the Stone Age if they continued to help him."

It was all slightly uneasy, but not that bad in Kunar Province. No one much wanted to fight the northern Pashtuns, and a lot of people were glad to see the troublesome Taliban out of the way, encamped somewhere south of Kabul. Waiting.

But then the unthinkable happened. On a lonely mountain road, near Asadabad, an air-to-ground missile fired from a US fighter jet hit and obliterated a white station wagon. The driver, his wife, and two children were all local. All Pashtuns. And they were all dead. And no one could understand why it had happened.

Whether or not the missile had killed them was a topic of vast speculation. There were rumors that the missile had slammed the vehicle off the road, and then a US patrol, believing the occupants to be Al Qaeda informants, or even spies, had opened fire and mowed down all four of them in cold blood, just as if Osama himself had been behind the wheel.

Missile or machine gun fire? That was an interesting question, but essentially not relevant. The rocket and/or the bullets were strictly American. And locally there was absolute outrage. It should be recorded that this time of massive US bombing all over the country was generally being kept under wraps. Or that was the way it seemed.

No one appeared to know how many US troops were near Asadabad, but there were some two thousand US military on the ground in or close to Afghanistan at the time. These included a thousand men of the Tenth Mountain Division—climbers and specialists in battles over rough terrain—still stationed at the US K2 Base across the northern border in Uzbekistan.

Shocking things were happening around this time. Afghan villages were being wiped out, north, south, east, and west, as the United States military ruthlessly sought out stragglers and activists still operating on behalf of the Taliban and Al Qaeda. Every couple of weeks, the little local radios reported the most terrible atrocities. There were estimates as high as three thousand civilians, including women and children, being killed during this US nationwide onslaught against the Taliban and Al Qaeda.

Everyone understood that the first casualty of war is usually the truth. But it did seem to the canny mountain tribesmen, in the long months following the 9/11 attacks, that the Americans were determined to nail anyone even associated with either terrorist organization. These activists would somehow be shot, bombed, or otherwise removed, with little regard for the "collateral damage": innocent people being killed in the cross fire.

The Pentagon policy, as relayed to the Afghan people, seemed to be "shoot or bomb first," however dubious the sources or information. Targets included cars and buses with unknown passengers. The aerial bombing took out probably hundreds of villages, from the White Mountains to the deep south of the country—based on reports of Al Qaeda or Taliban presence.

Everything seemed slightly remote from the Sabray area, and all of the information was second- or thirdhand—until the white station wagon. That stark and terrible incident was local. The occupants of that car were a completely innocent family known to many neighboring communities. None of the four had even the slightest connection to the Taliban.

News of the calamity spread rapidly across the mountains. It was a huge issue. Tribal councils were held, the elders conferred, village to village, and their leaders demanded explanations and apologies from the Americans. Gulab remembers the time well:

The sound of the mullah's call to prayers in the days immediately following the murders had a strange, mournful quality, and it resounded around the village. There were many sad faces during those days, and evenings, when we asked Allah to shine His light upon the souls of the four victims.

All of our dealings with the Americans were slow. At first, there were denials and evasions, and then they did finally apologize. But it was too late. Far, far too late. The mujahideen commanders had held a series of councils and considered the three Pashtunwali principles the American action had offended.

First there was number three, *badal*, or justice: the obligation to seek justice or take revenge against the wrongdoer. This carried no time limit. The insult can only be redressed by the shedding of the miscreant's blood. *Badal* often results in a blood feud lasting generations.

And then there was number four, *tureh*, or bravery—all Pashtuns being obliged to defend family and possessions against tyranny. Death must follow if anyone offends this principle.

Number ten was simply *nang*, or honor, and this stresses that all Pashtuns must defend the weak around them. Which included, of course, the four slain villagers in the burning car.

In a hundred tribal councils, all over the northern mountains, the Americans were found in breach of our sacred principles—reluctantly by the elders, since the USA was still our trusted friend and ally. Even more reluctantly, since they had stood with us in our battle to expel the Soviets.

Nonetheless, they were in breach. And the Afghani commanders, including my own brother, stood up and swore the ancient tribal oaths and vows. In those dark winter mountains, the mujahideen once more declared jihad against an occupying army: a former friend who had transgressed and appeared not to mind doing so again.

Holy war against the all-powerful USA was not an easy decision. But Pashtunwali does not seek what's easy. It seeks what's right. And our former brothers from the United States had overstepped our line of demarcation.

And the mujahideen cry of "Revenge!" echoed around our hills. "Death to the infidel!" We were at war with the United States of America.

Mujahideen commanders understood that to start recruiting and then to attack the forces of the United States of America was little more than a declaration of mass suicide. They knew beyond doubt that the Americans could wipe Afghanistan off the map at the touch of a button; furthermore, many of the mujahideen had been mostly inactive since the Russians left twelve years before.

They were simply not ready to fight a war against anyone, never mind against the United States. And despite many misgivings about the ruthless Taliban army, that was really the only trained fighting force Afghanistan had.

Every Pashtun village had its own private arsenal, with weapons stacked and stored after they'd been stolen from the Russians. But the hurt from that careless US attack on that local station wagon would not go away. And the village elders were calling the Taliban commanders and handing over their guns and ammunition, AK-47s, and rockets.

Everything was presented to the disliked fundamentalist army despite all the concerns about the Taliban's methods and radical interpretations of the Koran. The Taliban had long and powerful links to all of the villages, and the little clusters of houses, mosques, and pastures in the Hindu Kush made up a prime recruiting ground for the Taliban.

They would arrive at regular intervals and ask to speak to the young men, inspiring them with tales of great victories on the battlefield. And they stressed that Allah regarded them as the chosen people, and that He would protect them. In the event of death, they would be summoned into the Arms of Allah and cross the bridge into paradise, to the sound of the heavenly trumpets. Many virgins would await them.

Which probably sounded quite tempting to the new teenage recruits. Many of them accepted Taliban training and went with their new commanders to fight a foreign foe. All of this had a polarizing effect on village populations: there were families whose sons had gone to join the army, and others who did not approve of that army, its leadership, and its harsh and medieval intentions.

They certainly did not condone the presence somewhere in the mountain heights of the most wanted man on earth, Sheik bin Laden, gazing reproachfully at this nation while he provided the outlawed army of Taliban fighters with both Saudi cash and encouragement.

The Taliban had enemies not only within the villages but also in the cities and rural areas where they had, while in power, burned vast areas of fertile land and then withheld food supplies sent by the United Nations. The years of Taliban rule had been cruel and extreme, using terrorism to further their ideological and political intentions.

In so many ways, it was America that had liberated the country from this form of national tyranny. And yet the specter of the white station wagon hung over them all. Now the villages were at war with their once-trusted ally, and people like Gulab understood that they might be obliged to pick up the machine guns once more and begin the long road into the hills to try to ambush and kill the occupying foreigners. And they understood this would be a lot more complicated than fighting the Russians.

By now, the Lion of Sabray was twenty-eight years old, a veteran commander and gunnery officer, requiring no further training. People would always look to Gulab and his elder brother for solutions to the American problem.

However, the United States was a lot more elusive, and the mujahideen concentrated on guerrilla actions, seeking out US patrols in high hills, never taking them on in close combat. The Americans were so well armed, trained, and equipped, racing above the land in helicopters and warplanes, and relying on their smart bombs and missiles to do their damage.

The mujahideen stuck to subtle lightning attacks, watching for US helicopter troop landings, lying in wait for the disembark. If the US troops were not blown out of the sky with the remaining US-built Stinger missiles, the mujahideen would open fire as soon as American boots touched the ground. The Afghan rebels' task was to make their lands once more the most dangerous place on earth for any intruder.

Even almost four years after 9/11, there was still a polarization among the Pashtun people about the structure of this strange war. For some, especially those who had fought so hard against the Russians, the vision of that deep and friendly relationship with the United States was still in place. Congressman Charlie Wilson was a lot more popular than bin Laden.

But the apparition of that burning white station wagon remained.

Afghanis could not understand why the Americans had done this. They could not even understand why America was interested in Afghanistan. And the bombing of Tora Bora had scared them, because they thought they might be next.

They'd tried to believe that the good-hearted United States of America never wished to kill innocents. Then, quite suddenly, with that attack on local people, everything changed. But, curiously, they still could not raise the same venom for the Americans as they had for the Russians.

They had to accept that the United States had turned against them, but it was in a spirit of sadness rather than fury. Although the mujahideen leaders tried constantly to whip everyone into a frenzy, rekindling the hatreds of war, they were only partially successful.

The Taliban remained unpopular in many sections of the community. At first, they had been full of promise with their devout views on the Koran, but once in power, they had swiftly alienated half the population.

They'd infuriated people in the Hindu Kush by imposing a tax on profits in the timber business, collecting it ruthlessly. And they were worse in the cities, shooting and bombing Americans, with apparent disregard for the many, many Afghani citizens who were hit and killed in the cross fire.

For Gulab, the American war did not represent a call to arms, though Sabray was ready. He stayed busy in the timber business, earning a living and hoping that the United States would decide to leave, since Sheik bin Laden was plainly no longer a resident on the Afghani side of the Pakistan border.

He remembers well the night of June 27, when he awoke to the sound of what seemed to be a helicopter in the near distance:

I do not think military commanders from any war, no matter how distant, ever sleep quite so long and peacefully as civilian citizens. Definitely I don't. Somehow, deep in my subconscious, I hear again the murmur of the battlefield and the terrible anger of the guns.

Brought up, as I was, in the heart of a vicious armed conflict against a well-armed but less cunning enemy, I have never known true tranquility at night, and it's possible I never will.

The family had gone to bed early, soon after the sun had slipped behind the western peaks, and the long shadows of the mountain had enveloped the village. A bright three-quarter moon soon rose above the peaks, and I awakened, stood up, and found myself staring out the window into the darkness.

And then I heard something, which up there is very rare. I thought I could sense the faraway thumping of a helicopter engine, rising and falling on the summer wind, sometimes near and sometimes far. I think it was real, but perhaps not. I remember deciding it must be American, but it was very late, even for them.

There were no bombs, no explosions, no gunfire, and no scream of a Taliban missile howling out of its launcher. Nothing, really, except the half-real, distant *whop-whop-whop* of the rotors on a big helicopter several miles away. And then, quite suddenly, it grew fainter, and then vanished, and there was only silence.

I was tired, but suddenly I had no wish to sleep, and I stood there staring at the North Star, bright in the black northern heavens. This was the same bright star beloved of all battle commanders seeking the right direction while on the move in the night.

Around that time, it began to rain quite heavily. And if anyone was out there, on the mountain, I felt for them. The Hindu Kush uplands were no place to be in rough weather. They lacked shelter or any kind of cover, and they were swept for hours on end by winds made stronger by the sharp and steep escarpments.

The weather was one thing, but, as an Afghan officer would, I still kept wondering if I had been listening to a helicopter. And if so, what was it doing up here, probably forty-five minutes from the big US air base at Bagram? It had not come to bomb or strafe. So what had it come for? Perhaps an insertion of troops? US Special Forces?

But if so, where were the Al Qaeda or Taliban missile men? Why had I heard no shots, when I knew perfectly well there was a sizable Taliban army over in that direction? Perhaps I'd been mistaken. Maybe the American war had not, after all, come up here to our peaceful pastures just as summer had arrived.

I went back to bed but barely slept before the sun once more came up over the high peaks. We prayed soon after dawn, and I remember walking up to the village mosque in the quiet of the first light. I remember listening, I suppose, for another US helicopter, but there was no sound from the empty skies, and soon I was on my prayer mat in a crowded but holy room, alone with my own thoughts and with Allah.

I had much work to do in the timber business that day, and it would take me to the hills high above the village. All through that morning, Tuesday, June 28, I cut and stacked the hardwoods which had already been felled.

Perhaps this is with the benefit of hindsight, knowing what I now understand so much better, but I occasionally paused and strained my hearing for the sound of another helicopter. But there never was.

If the US military had been up there on a bombing run, or even one of its other missions of destruction, the population of Sabray would have known by now. The Americans were still liable to bomb a whole community just to take out a few Taliban or Al Qaeda warriors, and that was apt to be an impossibly noisy procedure.

If the Americans had landed a marauding Special Forces patrol, the Pashtuns would have known that before the mullah called the faithful to prayer that morning. But they'd heard nothing. So the question hung in the fresh mountain air: What was a US military helicopter doing up there in the middle of the night, if not delivering military personnel? And where were those personnel?

It was approximately one hour after noon in the mountains where Gulab was toiling, and the sun was still at its height. The air was hot and thin. No clouds. And loading timber was hard work. That was when he heard the first sounds of battle echoing back across the high pastures.

Everyone in or near Sabray heard the start of it: one solitary loud shot from a high-powered machine gun, bigger than any Kalashnikov. Then a pause. Then a barrage of gunfire. Gulab gathered his thoughts. The noise came from the northwest, from the direction of Ahmad Shah's Taliban army. Someone had engaged them in combat. That much was obvious.

And in Gulab's mind, it was equally obvious who that enemy was: it had to be the Americans. There was only one way they could have arrived up here, and that was by helicopter. By the sound of the raging battle, it must have been a very big helo, or maybe there had been two of them. But Gulab had heard only one.

He knew the United States had big Chinooks that could carry dozens of US military, and he believed that Shah had around four hundred armed warriors. Thus, in those moments, he estimated the Americans had a sizable force up there, and there would be a great deal of dying. The only thing that baffled him was the Americans' apparent willingness to fight without air cover. That was so unlikely.

So far as Gulab could tell, all the advantages were with the Taliban's mountain men—territorial experts. But with or without air cover, the sheer volume of the gunfire was astounding. He wondered many times about the fate of the young Pashtun men, doubtless being mowed down by heavy US firepower. Everyone had relatives in that Taliban army.

Anger toward the Americans was bad, but against the Taliban, it was equally vindictive. Basically, most Pashtuns disliked both combatants, but up here in the mountains, with a major military action in place, those old blood ties kicked in. No one would have cared if the Taliban disbanded, but in a firefight, they were the blood brothers, not the Americans. In the fight currently blasting away on the mountains, the men from the United States of America were the real enemy, from far away, no ifs, ands, or buts.

Gulab stood there in those high woodlands, listening to the staccato rattle of the guns; the rise and fall of the battle. By his assessment, maybe forty US inserted troops had come up here in the night and now faced the hordes commanded by Ahmad Shah.

The Taliban commander would probably take heavy casualties, but in the end, his cunning, stealthy fighters should overwhelm the US attack. Gulab tried to guess precisely where all this was happening, but that was difficult. So far as he could tell, it was about one and a half mountains away—probably seven miles—but in this light summer air, it sounded much closer.

He had no watch, no way to tell time, except for the sun. He estimated the battle lasted for around ninety minutes, with continuing sporadic fire.

At that point, it was almost entirely Kalashnikov gunfire he was hearing, with the occasional whoosh and scream of an RPG. There were already reports, rumors, and whispers of a sensational battle that had taken place all the way down the mountain.

There had been many Taliban casualties, possibly a hundred, against a small, highly trained group of US Special Forces, and the Taliban army was apparently still out there.

Sabray was getting some information, though certainly not all. And there was little news of exactly why the gunfire died down, with only a few RPGs still exploding. It seemed that whatever had been happening was over. Ahmad Shah had subdued whatever threat there was, but no one had an accurate picture of the action—only that many Afghanis had died.

As a Pashtun, Gulab is not a boastful man, but he has his skills and some knowledge, mostly of mountain warfare. Lacking formal education, he rarely claims expertise, except in two areas of the battlefield: gunfire and explosions. Inside the mujahideen, on those subjects, he is an acknowledged master.

But shortly before two o'clock on that hot June afternoon, Mohammed Gulab heard the thunderous roar of twenty-first-century conflict as he had never experienced before. It was a barrage of such intensity that he wondered how any enemy could possibly withstand it.

Out there in the timber country, the blasts came echoing through the mountains—one after another, sometimes in clusters where the explosions fused together. Up close, he thought, it must have sounded like an atom bomb, sufficient to destroy your hearing.

But they were not bombs. Gulab knew the sound of them. These were very noisy Russian-built RPG-7s—rocket-propelled grenades—designed to blow battle tanks in half. And he knew the Americans had no tanks up there, not in that steepest part of the mountains, and no vehicles, either.

But the Taliban did have the RPG-7. So they were using them against armed US personnel only. That much he could work out for himself. He also knew there could not be many Americans to fire at, since he'd heard only one helicopter, and this little battle was already nearly two hours old.

Gulab could discern the type of rockets being used: probably high-explosive fragmentation as well as thermobaric antipersonnel warheads, both capable of causing absolute havoc. Judging by the noise, they must have unleashed a hundred of them. Heaven help their enemy.

He could not imagine anyone living through that. They'd obviously taken an area where the Americans were making a stand and thrown everything they had at them. He could not know what the US troops had done, but there were a lot of very angry Taliban commanders over there. Gulab was pretty sure that survival would have been impossible.

The RPG-7 is deadly at two hundred meters, but the mujahideen rocket men were accustomed to getting in close, firing at eighty meters or less. And they understood accuracy. Against the Russians, they would fire and blow up Soviet tank tracks, and then go for the main armor.

The two US Army Black Hawk helos downed in Mogadishu, Somalia, in 1993 were hit by RPG-7 rockets. And the Taliban missile operators were a lot better than the Somalian terrorists.

Gulab waited up there on the mountain for the noise to subside and signify the end of this battle. Which it did, but only partly. There was still intermittent gunfire, so however much damage the grenade barrage had done, it had not destroyed the Taliban's enemy. Because they were still attacking someone. And again he wondered how many Americans had been on that mountain—and how many were left.

By now, the rumors were flying faster than the bullets. Up in the pastures, word was that half the Taliban force had been wiped out, but only one American body had been found. No one believed that, since that last heavy attack sounded great enough to have knocked down Kabul.

But the enormous, sustained barrage had died down—not out, just down. And the villagers were hearing that Taliban casualties were really bad, dozens and dozens lying dead or badly wounded on the mountain. And the sporadic gunfire continued, not like before, but enough to get Sabray's attention. Gulab remembers thinking he was hearing one of the most violent confrontations of the American war in the mountains. He was also listening to one of the most puzzling. After that massive barrage of rocket grenades, the air became still for a few minutes. Gulab thought it was over—the Taliban's enemies had plainly been wiped out.

But no, here it came again. More gunfire. Then rockets. Whoever had confronted Shah's forces was still fighting. Someone was still firing at something. And whatever that was, someone was firing right back. Gulab was brought up with the sound of the AK-47 ringing in his ears from the age of eight. He knew the difference. And the intermittent return fire he was hearing from over those mountains was unmistakably heavier US rifle fire.

By now, it was impossible even to try guessing the numbers involved. US intelligence had the number of Shah's Taliban fighters at a hundred or fewer, but Gulab insists that there were closer to four hundred men. No one knew how many of them had stepped up to the front line to face the Americans.

By around two o'clock, it was much quieter. He could still hear sporadic bursts, but nothing sustained until just before two thirty, with the sun very high. At that moment, there was a barrage of gunfire—AK-47s—as if they were letting fly at anything that moved; or, perhaps, searching for a target, somehow hoping to flush it out.

Whatever it was, there were a couple more rocket blasts, and then it all went very quiet, as if the battle had finally ended. The last scattering of shots were all from Kalashnikovs, no return fire. The Taliban, in Gulab's opinion, had eliminated their enemy.

But there remained, as ever, the twisting, turning, tribal contradictions, which had riven the dark hills of Afghanistan for two thousand years. And those ingrained fractures between ancient clashing empires, having evolved into modern disputes, made national government virtually impossible.

Tribal ethnic and language differences caused endemic tensions and led to blood feuds among Afghan warlords. These rumbled down the years, magnifying differences and eradicating the factors that ought to bind them together. In Sabray alone, there was still this schism separating families whose sons had gone to join the army of Ahmad Shah and those who regarded the Taliban commander with long-held suspicion.

Thus there were rival factions standing on opposite sidelines as that late June battle erupted on the nearby mountains. Some villagers prayed for their own families and rooted for the Taliban. But there were others hating the prospect of another Taliban rule and praying for the Americans to take them out. All in one village—could anything be more blindingly confusing than that?

And then, of course, there were people like Gulab: mujahideen loyalists who wanted nothing to do with any foreign invaders and nothing to do with the Taliban, either—brutal, unenlightened, religious imposters that they were.

For him, it was even more baffling. Raised as a battlefield commander, he could not quite decide whether American troops were still at large in these hills or not. And neither could he make up his mind why they had come in the first place. He simply believed the Taliban had probably finished them, by pure weight of numbers.

And then he heard a sound so familiar, it was like the soft tread of his youngest son. The noise came from far off to the east, clearly audible. It was one of those massive US Chinook MH-47s—an aircraft capable of transporting up to fifty military personnel, not including the pilot, copilot, and flight engineer—clattering up over the peaks.

When Gulab first heard it, that helicopter was flying straight and true—no stopping and starting like the US aircraft he'd heard late last night. This one was sure of its landing zone. Those big twin-rotor helos are essentially heavy lifters used for troop transportation. You want to move a fighting force, and fast, get a Chinook-47.

I strained to hear its direction better, turning my head sideways to the warm, early-summer wind, and then, suddenly, I heard yet another sound so familiar to me: the whoosh and whine of a Stinger missile followed by the instantaneous *kaboom!* of its sixty-one-pound hit-to-kill warhead. And then, seconds later, an almighty thumping crash on the mountainside, as several tons of heavy, burning steel and gasoline smashed into the ground.

I was astounded at the clarity, how I could hear it so plainly, but at this height in the high peaks, sounds are sometimes amplified by the echoing effect of the escarpments.

Obviously I was blind to all of this. But acute hearing and heightened sound in clear, silent air magnified it all. And I knew beyond doubt, that the Taliban rocket men had hit that Chinook, and there were many more dead on the mountain.

As sounds of the burning and explosives died away, there was again silence. Those Boeing rotors were stopped forever. And Allah alone knew of the forthcoming consequences of this. The United

States did not take military setbacks lightly, as Osama bin Laden would likely attest.

I stopped working for a few minutes, listening for further developments. But there was nothing, not even a few scattered gunshots from the Taliban AK-47s, which a veteran like myself could always distinguish.

Of course, among the Sabray timber men that afternoon, there were other experienced mujahideen troops, and, inevitably, we gathered to speculate. But it was so quiet up here, and there was little to be learned until the herders began to return through our lands, and then the rumors would begin in earnest.

I think we went home early, walking down to the village long before dark, and the only thing we noticed in the final couple of hours was heavily increased US air traffic: helicopters and fighter jets, clattering and screaming across the skies above the Hindu Kush.

To tell the truth, it was nerve-racking for us. Because we all understood how violently the Americans would react if the Taliban rocket men really had the temerity to knock a big US Chinook out of the sky. Hopefully, Sabray was just far enough away to be judged innocent of the "crime."

Aside from the many extra military flights over this part of the country, there was nothing to give the locals a clue about what had sparked the firefight. But they'd know a lot more as the evening wore on.

Gulab had no news update for several hours after daybreak. No one who arrived in Sabray knew anything more than anyone else.

The Taliban army still had only two American bodies, but they were celebrating the massacre of the US reinforcements in the downed helicopter.

He went up to the hills above the village to check three things: the timberlands, the pastures, and what Americans call the grapevine— that's the rumor system that works as well up there in the Hindu Kush as it does anywhere else.

He remembers the quiet of the morning, and his thoughts were of the many dead Pashtun tribesmen, his own people. Gulab had no time for the Taliban or for any of their wishes and ideals. But his own people had died yesterday up here on their own mountain, fighting against Americans.

And now there was only silence. And it went on for hours and hours. There seemed to be no one walking by with any information. And, so far as anyone knew, there were possibly two heavily armed American killers wandering around—men who had helped to wipe out half of Ahmad Shah's army.

"I was not afraid," says Gulab. "But I was careful, and I never took one step in any direction without my AK-47. There were three of us still patrolling the upper fields, walking slowly, when I heard, around the middle of the day, the unmistakable crack of a gunshot echoing across the escarpment, much closer than the rest of the battle sounds we had heard the previous afternoon. Like all ex-field commanders, I stopped breathing just for a second, awaiting the burst of return fire. But it never came. And from that, I was drawing a thousand conclusions.

"In my own mind, I was certain the shot I'd just heard was from a

Kalashnikov. Either they'd dropped an American dead in his tracks, or the man had surrendered. Or escaped. But they'd shot at something or someone. And no fire had been returned.

"Once more the mountains were silent. And they stayed that way for maybe an hour. And then, suddenly, considerably closer, there was an unbelievable explosion: an RPG-7, or even a hand grenade or a bomb. But the ground shuddered, and the aftershock echoed, and I guessed it was only about a mile away.

"The mystery deepened, because afterward there was only silence. Maybe they'd somehow killed each other! As my American friend frequently remarks, 'Beats the hell out of me!'

"And more time passed—maybe another couple of hours—during which I had no idea what was happening."

It might have been quiet up in the high pastures above the village, but there was chaos on the steep slopes where Petty Officer M. Luttrell was still battling for his life and struggling to find water. Gulab recalls:

I was walking down toward the river with my two friends on our way back to the village, when I noticed a sudden unusual movement away to our left, in a small, rocky area near the water.

At first, I saw only a dark shape, and I thought it might be a mountain lion, although it was going pretty slowly and moving very low to the ground. Also, it was headed into a wide crevasse, which I knew was a dead end. No lion could leap out of there, not up and across twenty-foot-high rocks. Lions are not normally that dumb.

I raised my rifle and told one of my two companions to do the same, and quietly we advanced to the mouth of the wide gully. In just a few strides, we could see our problem. This was no lion. Right here we had a huge US Special Forces warrior, with a black beard and a serious-looking machine gun—bigger than our Kalashnikovs. And he was aiming it straight at me.

I yelled out a warning and ducked left behind a tree, and my friends also dived out of the way. That American rifle could have gunned down all three of us, handled by this Special Forces man. He wouldn't miss.

Essentially, we were being confronted by one of the most dangerous combat marksmen in the world, and I was sure of my ground here. US troops are generally banned from wearing beards, except for SEALs and other Special Forces, whose duties often required them to fraternize with tribal enemies of the United States. This giant had a beard like Fidel Castro, and he must have stood six feet six inches tall, and that rifle was loaded.

From the back of the tree, I yelled at my friends to take great care and not to get in this monster's line of fire. I shouted that I would try to talk to him and tell him we meant him no harm.

I peered out from behind my tree and was immediately struck by two new facts: he appeared to be either asleep or unconscious—maybe wounded—and he did not have any trousers. I also could see a lot of blood on his face and left leg.

I raised my rifle and came slowly out from behind the tree. But suddenly this terrible man came alive, pushed himself into firing position, rammed that big rifle into his shoulder, and took aim.

I shouted at him to calm down, but he was an American fighting machine, like all of those characters from the SEALs, and I ducked back behind my tree as fast as I've ever done anything.

I kept yelling at him, "Taliban? No Taliban!"

And suddenly he answered, "No Taliban!" And I jumped out from the back of the tree and pulled my open palm across my throat, trying to signal "death to the Taliban." And I shouted again, "No Taliban!"

He plainly did not believe that because he swung his rifle straight at me, which caused me to duck into cover with record speed. I would take no chances with this man. None whatsoever. But when I next risked a glance, he was again asleep. And somehow I knew we were dealing with a very seriously injured soldier.

In the bright afternoon sun, I could see blood on the rocky ground beneath him, and slowly I ordered my two companions to come out. We put down our guns and walked up to him with our arms held wide out in front of us, in that universal signal of friendship.

But again he came to life, pushed himself up, and aimed that rifle. I ordered my two friends to stand quite still and keep our arms wide, to convince him we would not attack him.

At that moment, he seemed to surrender, let go of his rifle, and tried to open his arms in submission. Too late. He blacked out completely.

And I walked toward him and stood over him, and I thought he was dead. I could see where he had somehow wept, by the marks down his cheeks. I could see how much he had been hurt. His injuries were still bleeding, vividly, on his face. He was deathly pale. I was certain he was dying.

"Who are you?" I asked loudly.

And very slowly, his eyes opened, and he looked directly at me, no longer as a rabid enemy but as a man who'd traveled far—as far he could possibly go. And his head fell back on his rocky pillow. And blood streamed down his face, and I could see shards of metal jutting from his shattered left thigh.

Just before he blacked out again, his voice croaked. And with terrible difficulty, he said, "My name is Marcus. I'm an American."

- 4 -

INTO THE ARMS OF ALLAH

It was hard for me to understand the man's words. But I did think he said his name was Marcus. I was also fairly certain he was dead, right there at my feet, still bleeding. I actually thought he had a gentle face, and I knew he was someone's greatly loved son; perhaps a brother or even a husband.

In a sense, I suppose he was my enemy, although I understood the Americans were out to get Al Qaeda, not just regular Afghani citizens. And, in another way, I disliked the Taliban a lot more than I hated this mortally wounded American.

Instinctively, I thought I'd just seen his dying moments. And I stood there watching him: this giant, bearded warrior.

What happened next was perhaps the great turning point in my life. I leaned over and touched the left-hand side of his neck, feeling for a pulse. And quite suddenly, a bright light surrounded him. I have no idea whether anyone else could see it, but I did, and it was clear, and it formed a kind of protective shield around him.

Simultaneously, I felt something in my heart: not the kind of emotion one usually feels for a shot enemy combat soldier, but the kind of feeling which might be reserved for an injured brother or a child.

And then, for the first time in my life—the only time, before or since—I heard, quite distinctly, the voice of Allah, coming to me in resonant tones.

And I have not the slightest doubt what was said. With the light still bright and glowing around the stricken Marcus, I heard: *"You must guard and protect this American. Mohammed Gulab, you will keep him safe."*

I almost went into shock. I can't imagine what my two companions thought, because I was in some kind of a trance, listening to a command from another place; a command which could have come only from God.

It's hard for me to explain the confusion of this situation. The American was an infidel, an armed enemy in our lands, and however much we disliked the Taliban, we were all Islamist, as we had been for more than a thousand years.

There were no circumstances in which I could reasonably be requested to help an infidel who had invaded our nation and our country. In my opinion, he'd also killed many, many members of Ahmad Shah's army. Surely he had to be one of the four Americans the Taliban leader had identified, two of whom were dead?

And here he lay, at my feet, desperately wounded, hovering between life and death, plainly being hunted by my own Afghani people, the ones who sympathized with the Taliban. My God! The almighty, all-knowing Allah had spoken to me in person and ordered me to help and guard this enemy of our people.

My mind raced. I tried to think of another place, perhaps another being who might have deceived me. But there was no other explanation. This was an order from Allah. The highest power in this world, and beyond, had chosen me to protect Marcus.

The command was as bewildering as it was unique. How was I supposed to communicate this strange situation to my companions and also to the villagers of Sabray? It flashed through my mind that no one would believe me. I am not an Imam. Indeed, I am a well-known mujahideen field commander, machine gunner, lifelong soldier, defender of the status quo here in our mountains.

I am devout in my beliefs, I pray five times a day, and I am in communication when necessary with the Prophet. However, neither he nor Allah has ever communicated with me directly. That is not the Muslim way. We offer our prayers, and the Imams are always here to advise us. And now this. A brand-new role for the Lion of Sabray.

I stared down at the American, and the light was still around him. And suddenly he opened his eyes and looked right at me. In his face I saw pleading, unspoken but very evident. And in those fleeting moments, I understood why I had been commanded by Allah. In truth, I did not totally comprehend why, but I did realize the very definite nature of my task.

God had chosen me. Of that I was certain. My duties would be fraught with danger, and they would surely declare me the enemy of the Taliban. But I have commanded armies in these hills, and I am not afraid of the followers of Ahmad Shah.

In my soul, I felt only humility, and I felt very sure of myself and my obligations. If anyone wanted to kill him, they must kill me first. These were moments which would change my whole life. I did not seek them. I certainly did not ask for them.

The message had come from Allah, and Allah is great, and there is no other God. As I looked down on Marcus, I knew one thing: there was nothing on this earth that would have induced me to change my mind. For I fear only Allah, and for whatever reason, He had chosen me.

In my eyes, at least, the bright light still glowed around the man. I had yet to address one word to him personally except for "No Taliban!" But first I needed to speak to my companions, one of whom was our village doctor—a relatively skilled medical man who had learned his craft on the battlefield of the Hindu Kush in the Russian war. His name was Dr. Sarawar.

I half expected both him and the other villagers to ask me whether I had suffered some kind of mental collapse since I had not spoken for several minutes. But it was as if time had stood quite still. They picked up our previous conversation as if there had been no intervention between myself and Allah, as if mere seconds had elapsed since the soldier had let go of his rifle.

Sarawar never even suggested he'd also seen the light that illumi-

nated the injured man. So I did not mention it, either. That was between Allah and me, and perhaps the American.

But now the light faded. And, plainly by the grace of Allah, the
man seemed infused with a new surge of life. And he was speaking
in a completely foreign language and trying to signal to us, holding
up his fist loosely and opening his mouth.

Dr. Sarawar tuned in and suddenly called out, "Ahh! Hydrate!" at
which point I couldn't tell what either of them was trying to communicate, since I cannot speak one word of English. But I saw the man
nod his head quickly, and Sarawar sent someone to fill a big water
bottle from the pool. By now, we'd been joined by three other people
from Sabray.

For some reason, the wounded man suddenly laughed. Which surprised me, because I had never met anyone with less to laugh about
than he had. Flat on his back, he was glugging the water and chuck-
ling. Years later, Marcus told me through an interpreter that he just
could not believe this "crazy-assed tribesman who only spoke in long
words!" My friend Dr. Sarawar was one of the most educated men in
the village.

But he seemed to relax, trying to speak to us, and I sensed no
more hostility from him. He wasn't planning to mow us down with
that big American machine gun anymore. He was a lot more interested in staying alive, and he was worried about that gaping wound
on the back of his left thigh, which was still oozing blood onto the
ground. In my view, the bullet was still in there, and that was not
good. However, Sarawar would know what to do.

Meanwhile, the senior men—myself, the doctor, and one other—needed to go into conference. So we sent a couple of kids over to talk to the American, and even from a distance, I could see how well he got along with them. I kept hearing them shouting with laughter, which was not bad, considering none of them could understand a word of what the other was saying.

I later learned that the issue was the long fall down the mountain which had carried him straight past the pool, and then caused him to climb all the way back up. I could see them jumping up and down, like kids do, and I could hear them yelling at him in Pashtun: "Ha! Ha! Ha! You fall long way like a lunatic—very funny trick on the mountain. Everyone saw you—everyone laughing at hopeless mountain man!"

It obviously hurt the man to laugh. But he was very nice to them, and they somehow communicated with him. Even from afar, I found it moving. And for me it cast a new light on this great brute I was now sworn to protect.

But for now, his sudden arrival had caused a problem for me and my friends, and ultimately for the people of Sabray. The issues, for a Pashtun mountain man, were so far-reaching, they were almost overwhelming. And they involved a decision which must be made, and made quickly—because without the intervention of Allah, peace be upon him, Marcus would, in my opinion, have died. And may yet do so without help from us.

He had nothing left, no strength, and he was bleeding to death. Our water bought him some time, but not much—not without medical attention.

And now he lay on the ground, helpless on this rocky riverbank above the village. And the issues involved the deepest obligations of the Islamic religion, the highest possible moral consideration, and the always-present virtue of mercy. I am dealing with the ancient two-thousand-year-old principles of Pashtunwali, the graces of which must guide our every waking day.

This was unspoken but universally understood among the men who would now retire to make a decision. I would take the lead, and Sarawar would speak almost certainly in support of my views. As with doctors the Muslim world over, his instinct was always mercy, under the guidance of Allah. The other two men, lifelong friends, would be free to offer whatever opinions they might have.

I offered a wave of friendship to Marcus, which he probably did not understand, and we walked just a few paces nearer the water, leaving him alone with the kids, who were, incidentally, still laughing.

We all understood what we must decide, but I should explain briefly what was at stake. One of the bylaws of Pashtunwali is that if we should take in this stranger from the United States and help him and feed him and provide him with fresh water, then that imposes upon us an obligation which cannot be broken.

And that obligation, in the eyes of the Prophet, required us all—the entire village—to defend him to the death; to defend him, if necessary, until there was no one left alive. I already had that obligation, placed upon me by Allah Himself, but that was private between me and my Creator.

For the rest of my fellow citizens, the issue was extremely serious.

Because this was no small matter. This was clad in iron shackles. There was indeed a heavily armed enemy standing right before us: Ahmad Shah's battered Taliban army.

And they would want the death of the American more than they had ever wanted anything—except, perhaps, for the severed head of President George W. Bush. They would stop at nothing in order to grab him from us and execute him, probably on video.

To help him, to take him home with us, was to force my village and all of its people into a declared war with the Taliban. The slightest semblance of assistance to this wounded enemy would signify a brand-new set of rules for all of us.

For there were ten great principles of Pashtunwali—and six of them applied directly to the saving of the man. And I was sworn to obey them in my private, sacred covenant with Allah. And this I had to explain to Sarawar and my other two friends, before they would lift one finger to help the American.

It would be bitterly unfair for me to try to "finesse" the problem past them, underplaying the deep and terrible consequences which may befall everyone—like an armed gunfight around the village.

I had to be straightforward and honest. I had to explain the commands I had received from the One and Only God, and I had to hope that goodness and mercy would prevail. The alternative was to walk away from him and leave him here to die under the hot afternoon sun, his remains soon to be eaten by wild animals.

Well, they could do that. Allah, so far as I knew, had not commanded the entire village to His holy purpose. Just me. And I already understood the ramifications of that. They could walk away if they chose. I could not.

I told the other three I had received a private message from Allah, and this was treated with respect. No one in Sabray took the words of the One and Only God with any cynicism. My revelation was treated as an iron-clad truth which ought to be obeyed, especially since Allah had very obviously stepped in and prevented the soldier from dying. We had all witnessed his sudden resurgence from his unconscious state.

It was impossible for us to walk away from the wounded American without trampling over the time-honored laws of our people. Pashtunwali was the creed of our lives. My friends *could* leave him to die, and perhaps escape the obligations. But not one of the other three was keen to risk offending Allah to this extent. Not after hearing the sternness of his words to me.

And, in great fear of our God, we bowed our heads in prayer and then walked over to where the soldier lay. And together we leaned over and gently helped him to his feet. He couldn't stand, and so we gripped hands and lifted him into a kind of "chair."

Very slowly, we set off down the mountain, toward Sabray. I doubted he would ever know the momentous decision we had made on his behalf, committing our tribal village to a possible war against the Taliban.

At this very moment, when we lifted him and gave him more water, the situation was settled. It came under the heading of *melmastia,* hospitality. He was no longer an enemy, nor even a hostile combatant. He was a visitor, a guest, and we could not, would not, allow him to be harmed by anyone.

I probably understood better than anyone that this would not be unanimously accepted by everyone in the village. Certainly the majority would follow the lead offered by Sarawar and me: the path of mercy and decency involving a badly wounded person who had done us no harm.

But those blood ties between certain families and the Taliban were strong, and there would be those who might consider that our actions bordered on the fringes of madness. Why would we even dream of endangering the lives of all our people just to save the life of this American monster we did not even know?

The fight of the Taliban army against the small band of US Special Forces was by now well known, even though it was only a day old. And there was no doubt that Marcus had been right in the thick of it. Plus, he looked to the tribesmen as if he could wipe out an entire army with his bare hands.

While the merciful instincts of Gulab and Sarawar had prevailed on the mountain, it was still to be seen if they would prevail down in the village. It is simply not the Pashtun teaching to act in a cruel and heartless manner, ignoring all forms of humanity; however, there may be an exception for an enemy who had occupied their country. Would the American soldier be seen as an invader akin to the Russians, or would he be viewed in more favorable light, like the Pashtuns used to have for their US allies?

We set off down the steep slope, and immediately I could see we had a problem. There were one or two younger men coming up to the pastures. It was still hot, around four o'clock, and as they passed, I could see a quizzical look on their faces, and as they stared at Marcus, I could see it change to one of acute dislike.

I do not think they yet understood the full ramifications of Pashtunwali, but they knew one thing: two very senior members of the village council were carrying an obvious infidel into the very heart of the Pashtun community.

It was entirely possible that these men had relatives who fought for Ahmad Shah. It was even possible they themselves planned to join that grand adventure at the earliest opportunity.

None of the young men would have dared question the wisdom of men like Sarawar and myself. Respect for the elders is drummed into all of our youth, and the doctor and I were both in our early thirties. That was a lot older than seventeen, and we both had high reputations: the battlefield commander and the learned doctor. No one was challenging our decisions. Islam does not treasure its youth like it recognizes its wise men. But the kids were not happy.

One hundred yards later, it happened again. This time I noticed the American glaring right back at their scowling expressions. And this time I turned around to see them pointing directly at our new guest.

It would take some time, no doubt, before I could convince him there would be many people in Sabray who wished him no harm and would not tolerate anyone else wishing him harm, either. Despite the West's often hostile view of all Islamists, there are very good people among us, as, of course, there are among every nationality.

He was obviously in terrible pain, and I spoke to Sarawar about relieving it somehow. His opinion was we had to make a major improvement in the condition of his blasted leg, which was peppered with shrapnel, rock, and wood splinters, still bleeding, infected, and causing him agonizing pain.

And we had to get that bullet out of the backside of his left thigh. Sarawar had excellent antiseptic cream, and we had ancient tribal herbs which he believed would make our new guest much more comfortable. Also, the soldier was in desperate need of more water. Sarawar said he'd rarely seen a man more dehydrated.

Even on that slow and, for him, painful journey down to the village, he blacked out twice more. I remained uncertain about whether we could keep him alive. But my orders were categorical. I must protect him.

I mentioned this briefly to Sarawar, who said he understood and seemed reluctant to have me elaborate further on the words delivered by Allah. But he had known me long enough to realize I was not inventing it. What I said, had happened. He did not doubt that.

When we reached the top houses in the village, the ones on the highest part of the northwestern gradient, I noticed he was again asleep; either that, or dead. I was not sure. A small crowd watched us as we made our slow progress, and I noticed a few wary looks. I was glad the man did not notice.

Finally, we reached the house, and we lowered him to the ground. I sent a couple of kids to bring out a cot, and we transferred him. He looked relieved, lying there, eyes now open, exhausted as only wounded combat troops can be.

But this was not a bed. This was an operating table. Sarawar brought over a hose and handed it to him to drink from.

We were more or less powerless to stop the village people from crowding around to watch, and, anyway, I did not want to antagonize anyone further. So we allowed them to stay, and Sarawar immediately went to work on that bullet wound.

Quickly he found not just the entry wound but also the exit hole. The Taliban marksman's shot had gone straight through the soldier's upper leg, and the injury was bleeding from both places. No wonder he had looked so deathly pale. He was still losing a lot of blood.

Sarawar cleaned the bullet wound, treated it as best he could, then got started on the ripped, torn, and shredded thigh. He washed it off, and I watched the man almost faint with pain as Sarawar touched the shards sticking out. But he never uttered a sound.

That was one brave man. And then the doctor selected a surgical instrument and began pulling out the splinters.

Some of the wood on the old hillside trees is centuries old and as hard as granite. The soldier had a whole bunch of these splinters slammed into his leg, clearly from a rocket blast. It happens when a tree trunk is blown to smithereens and the fractured wood flies everywhere. A big piece can kill a man, or even two. The little bits are like flying bullets, and I'd seen injuries of this kind before. It was not pretty.

But Sarawar worked on, meticulously pulling the debris out of the leg, washing away the blood, applying antiseptic cream. Finally, he applied a dressing, and we fetched the American some soft, clean Afghani clothes, two sets: white for day, black for night.

We helped him undress, pulled off his shirt, and that was when I received my next big shock. Right across his back and down his arms was a huge tattoo: a blue-black design with weird shapes. That really scared everyone, because it looked like some kind of voodoo; some tribal symbol of war with its circular lines, jagged edges, and spiked prongs on a weapon which looked suitable for the devil.

I also noticed there were three numbers tattooed onto him. I still remember them, *two-two-eight*. To my very unpracticed eye, the American numbering looked like two snakes standing in front of an entwined emblem signifying, to us, approaching attack—or even death.

That tattoo could have gotten him killed, and people were very nervous. Perhaps sensing this, the man began to tell Sarawar, who understood a few words of English, that he was a doctor.

Doctor! I never saw anyone look less like a doctor in my life. This huge, bearded man, carrying a big loaded machine gun, with a spare ammunition magazine, a hand grenade fitted into his gun belt, battle-field injuries—including a gunshot wound, a split forehead, a broken nose—and a tribal marking, signifying all-out war. On somebody.

Somehow he communicated to Sarawar that he was a special battlefield doctor sent up here by the Americans to tend to the wounded. There was, however, not so much as a stethoscope, or even a Band-Aid, in his possessions; just the machine gun and ammunition.

"Dr. Marcus," he kept saying. And he said it so often, even the kids learned it. I could see them all jumping up and down, laughing, and yelling, "Hello, Dr. Marcus! Hello, Dr. Marcus!"

The entire village gathering was relieved when they pulled Afghan clothes on the American soldier, obscuring that huge tattoo, and made him comfortable. Three of them carried his cot back inside for the night and helped him to lie down again. They brought him some food, which he did not much like: just flat bread, and warm goat's milk, which he rejected out of hand. But he liked the bread and drank some tea. By the time Marcus Luttrell was ready to sleep again, he looked a lot better than when he was first discovered by Gulab and his companions.

The temperature up there in the Hindu Kush frequently drops around 50 degrees from the searing heat of the day to the mid-30s at night. So Gulab put a couple of blankets over "Dr. Marcus" and then decided to go to the village mosque. This was important to him, because he had obviously made some important decisions since last he prayed. He walked to their most holy place and found it open but deserted.

Gulab took a prayer mat and tried to communicate with Allah

that he had done His bidding; that he had gathered friends and saved the American. Marcus was now in their care and relatively safe from harm. His injuries were clean and treated, and they had fed him and provided fresh water.

The collective obligation to protect him was a holy instruction, but it had come to Gulab alone, which gave him a special responsibility. He took it extremely seriously, and prostrated himself before his God, and prayed for the soul of Marcus, the infidel. He actually did this several times a day as long as they were together. That was his duty as an Islamist, well within the command of Allah. Of that Gulab was certain.

When he left the mosque, he gathered up his rifle, checked the magazine, and took a quiet walk around in the dark. He was back in field commander mode, senses alert, surveying the surrounding mountains—especially to the north, the steep slope nearest to where Shah's army was camped.

That was where he first noticed a light, possibly a lantern, moving. Then another. In his mind, there was no doubt. The Taliban were moving onto that escarpment, from which they could keep a twenty-four-hour watch on Sabray. They had discovered, even faster than Gulab expected, that the American soldier, their ultimate quarry, was in the village. He already knew they would stop at nothing in order to capture him, dead or alive.

In one way, he understood their fury. This man was one of only four US Special Forces who had wreaked total havoc on Shah's army. But Allah's disapproval of the murder of both innocents and prisoners of war is a basic rule of right or wrong in the teachings of the Koran. No Imam approves of willful murder. The children of the Hindu Kush were all taught that from childhood. It was simply unacceptable, and everyone knew it was wrong.

There is no passage in the Koran that gives anyone permission to go around killing people. The Koran stands tall as the final arbiter— and for Taliban warriors to enter Sabray and execute this wounded American, to whom the people were extending *melmastia*, that was out of the question.

Gulab's view was, if anyone wanted to kill the American, that would prove a lot more difficult than they thought. However, he did not underestimate their anger and determination. Which was why they were all parked out there on the mountain, awaiting their chance.

By now, it was very dark, with heavy clouds overhead and no moon. Gulab called at one or two houses of close friends and sought the latest information. It seemed there were four youngish men in Sabray who believed that the man should be handed over.

This was no surprise, since all four of them were known informers to the Taliban. They were dangerous because they could reveal precisely where the American was. At this time, Ahmad Shah's men knew, somehow, that he was in residence, but they did not know exactly where.

They could have conducted house-to-house searches, but that was tantamount to war. The people were not afraid of them, and if they had to, they'd fight, and Sabray was well armed.

Gulab believed they would stand behind him. Because there was a natural respect for a proven mujahideen field commander. That respect for his family lived on from the distant days when another generation had revered the words of his learned father.

Once back outside in the little main street, Gulab moved into cover and again scanned the mountainside. He kept well out of range of the Taliban guards' Russian night vision glasses. Nonetheless, he could still see the lights on the mountain, and he knew the enemies of the American were biding their time.

Gulab was a battle commander again, and he decided that the Taliban fighters would be preoccupied with their new encampment and highly unlikely to attack the American tonight. They could not possibly know which house he was in, although they might find out tomorrow from their informers.

But for now, Gulab judged Marcus as safely locked away and in no particular danger. He had taken the precaution of hiding Marcus's rifle; if the Taliban somehow broke into the house and discovered him, it would be one less thing to identify him as the wanted soldier. Neither he nor Sarawar, who could easily tell that Marcus was no doctor, gave much credence to the physician cover story, but maybe the clothes they put him in would slow down the Taliban. Although he'd already detected one or two shadowy figures moving furtively in the village, he elected not to visit Marcus again until the morning and went inside to join his family. At his own front door, he looked out to the mountain and saw once more lanterns, just two moving, with traces of a campfire, at a slightly higher elevation.

It was a comfortable house, thoroughly waterproof, with glass windows, an iron stove, a thick, loose-weave Afghan rug on the floor, and a heavy padlocked box containing valuables.

They slept on cots and piles of those huge Afghan cushions that have been a part of local households since ancient times. Gulab arranged for two of his sons to check on Marcus during the night and again in the morning. There was nothing urgent.

Gulab's view that Marcus would be safe until dawn was a tactical error, as the Taliban struck almost immediately.

Tipped off by the Sabray informers, who sneaked out to the mountain shortly after dark, Shah now knew where the infidel was holed up.

And they came for him in the early evening, awakening no one, just storming into the house where Marcus was sleeping. No one heard anything, but the door was quite heavy and fit tightly. They gave it a hefty kick and then swarmed into his room.

They knocked Marcus around, punching and kicking him while he lay on his cot, unable to stand. Not surprisingly, they aimed their hardest kicks at his bandaged left thigh.

They also used a rifle butt to deliberately break the bones in his wrist but stopped short of killing him either out of fear or respect for the village's mujahideen soldiers. They also knew enough English to taunt him with the news that they had downed a US helicopter, killing everyone on board. And that he was next. They planned to take him outside and cut off his head, publicly.

The Taliban "warriors" even invited some young local kids to enter the house and take turns punching the Navy SEAL. One saving grace of Marcus's not having the strength to defend himself is that if he had harmed the kids, this would have probably been enough of an excuse for the Taliban to shoot him right there.

The commotion quickly awakened the entire village, and Gulab was alerted. He saw what was happening and realized there was no point charging in there, gun blazing. There were just too many of them: eight in the room, plus more patrolling outside around the house, and hundreds hidden on the mountain.

There was only one way to solve this. And that was to summon the village elder, Gulab's brother-in-law, Maluk, a very senior and most respected man, around seventy-five years of age and married to his oldest sister, Shina.

Gulab explained the situation to him, and Maluk dressed quickly, while Shina made tea, which she poured into a glass resting in a silver holder. The small, bearded man brought it to the American, entering the room with immense dignity. Gulab, armed with his rifle and accompanied by two friends, stood guard at the door.

Maluk spoke quietly to the Taliban troops, who all stood up and stepped away from Marcus, nodding respectfully to Sabray's village elder. This deference was the complete opposite of the Western cult of soft hero worship, which does not exist up there in the Afghan mountains. No one in the entire country commands esteem for talents such as acting or singing.

Afghani warriors pay such "children" scant attention, reserving their respect and admiration for those who have experience, people who have seen much and learned life's lessons in the fields of politics and brave military command.

Gulab saw each Taliban fighter in Marcus's room step back and offer a short bow to Maluk, a man they could easily have killed, but would not dare to raise a finger against.

In the Hindu Kush, you must *earn* that degree of personal respect. It's a matter of power. Maluk commanded obedience from two or three other villages. Because here was a man who had led mujahideen battalions in the mountains against the invading Russians twenty years previously.

This was a man who had sat on a thousand village councils and been consulted by the Afghanistan government. He was not required to sing or shout. When the elder speaks, the rest of the room goes quiet. One critical word from him could end all forms of cooperation for traveling Taliban armies and recruiters.

Maluk's entrance clearly communicated that Marcus was under the protection of this village. And they could not dare upset the elder.

They probably also thought twice about threatening Gulab. He and Maluk were from the same family, and many assumed that Gulab would one day take his brother-in-law's place. Certainly, if they already knew that Marcus had been assigned to his personal care, they would have been wary about risking Gulab's anger.

Maluk's intervening instantly ended whatever forms of torture they were inflicting upon the American. He spoke quietly and calmly to them, and then he walked out, and the villagers formed a guard for his return home. Within moments, every one of the intruders left, walking up the hill to the north, back into the mountains, leaving Marcus very bruised and bleeding, but alive.

Gulab conferred with Sarawar, who returned to the house and re-dressed Marcus's wounds, while he went with Maluk to seek his advice. There were no doubts about the next move: they had to get the American out of that house and into hiding somewhere else. The elder felt that the Taliban were capable of sending a new raiding party once they guessed that Maluk had returned to sleep. But they would not defy him directly.

The villagers then formed a kind of battlefield stretcher party, returned to the house, and tried unsuccessfully to communicate to Marcus what was going on. He was utterly confused, but he did not resist being hauled out of bed and lifted outside. Sarawar held the lantern. It was about two o'clock in the morning.

They were headed to the most secure place in the village: a cave where they stored stolen Russian weaponry, high explosives, and ammunition. The strength of the cave was its secrecy, shielded as it was by thick bushes and set back into the trees. You could search for a hundred years and never find it. It was one of Sabray's assets, a place unknown to outsiders; a refuge for villagers who had some-thing to hide.

They made slow progress down the mountain, half carrying, half shouldering the huge Navy SEAL, who was nothing like the dead-weight he had been when they first brought him in.

Marcus was regaining his strength. With help, he could stand and nearly take a few steps. Trouble was, he was so much bigger than everyone else, and the journey was plagued by this physical imbalance. However, they managed to help him down to the banks of the local river, and this required a major decision. They had to get him across, and the riverbed was uneven and a bit slippery beneath the rushing mountain torrent of water.

But Marcus was Gulab's "guest," and he elected to carry him alone. He crouched, and they set Marcus in position. Gulab stood up, bearing the weight, and walked into the flowing stream. The American was one hell of a burden, but the Lion braced himself, gritted his teeth, and hauled him like a decorated elephant carrying an Indian rajah on his throne.

Step by step, he waded through the stream, knowing that if he stopped, they'd both end up in the water. He never faltered, just kept heaving, gripping Marcus's massive legs with two hands.

"I just knew he was trying not to laugh," Gulab says in retrospect. "It seemed like a long way, farther than it had ever been before, but we made it. And somehow I climbed the bank, and my troops rushed forward to help once we were on dry land.

"I had never before been required to hoist a weight like that. Not even in the timber-felling country. And I was certain I never would again. At least, not for a couple of days, when I was near certain I'd have to carry him back.

"He knew what I'd done. And he offered me a handshake on that riverbank. We couldn't speak, but he meant this gesture of his gratitude, and I've always remembered it.

"This warm note of friendship was perhaps our first, between two new friends, separated by the isolation of language, but by nothing else. Little did either of us realize it was a bond of great trust which would last for many, many years."

The gradient up to the cave's entrance was steep. But they pushed and hauled the giant SEAL until finally they stood at the entrance. This was no hotel, but they did try to clear some of the small rocks and fix a place for Marcus to lie down, inside the cave and away from the entrance. In their haste to exit the village house, they had brought no food or water. But they found an old Pepsi bottle, and Gulab went down to the river to fill it for him.

By now, it was four o'clock in the morning, not yet light and still moonless. The team members began to disperse, making their way through the dark and back down to the river. Gulab stayed awhile with Marcus until he fell asleep, and then he crept out of the cave and positioned himself to the left of the entrance. He stood guard there until dawn, his AK-47 primed and loaded.

"The thing was," he says, "I did not trust those Taliban for one split second, and neither did I know whether they'd observed our evacuation party moving through the night and across the river. If they had, I was certain they'd come calling very soon. And so I just sat there, fulfilling my obligation to Allah. One sight of a Taliban advance on our cave, I'd open fire. And I was trained long ago not to press the trigger until I couldn't miss.

"My mission on this dark night had its own perimeters. Once stationed at the entrance to the cave, I needed to stay there. Because someone could be watching. It was entirely feasible the Taliban may have spotted me clambering into the bushes, and I dared not desert my post in case they decided to rush into my area and then execute Marcus. So I just stayed until long after dawn.

"Soon after 0800, the goat-herders arrived, climbing up the hill to pastures which began above the cave. I'm sure the tinkling bells around the animals' necks awakened Marcus, but I still did not want to leave the entrance. I'd wait for Sarawar and the rest of my team to arrive later in the morning, at which point I'd post a new guard, who would be a member of my family.

"I actually chose my brother Haji Nazer Gul, the fearless mujahideen warrior in his day. He was whip thin, abnormally strong, and afraid of no one. By trade, he was a mountain machine gunner like me. Only to such a man would I entrust the life of Marcus. Nazer is a devout Islamist, and one of the few people to whom I had confided my vision of Allah's bright light around the injured American."

The sun was quite high when Sarawar finally arrived. He came with several friends, and they brought fresh dressings for Marcus's wounds and freshly baked bread and water. And while they worked to make him feel better, Gulab walked home, down the mountain and over the river. He was tired by now, and ahead of him was another long night. He remembers:

With Haji Nazer Gul on duty outside the cave, I was confident our guest would be safe. And by this time, all of my friends and allies in the village knew about the clandestine American in my care. I had spoken sternly to many of them, explaining how certain I was that the American's life was important to Allah.

There was nowhere in the Koran which stated Pashtunwali applied only to those of the Muslim faith. Certainly there was nothing to suggest that hospitality be withheld from infidels. In fact, it was quite the opposite. This was a matter of right and wrong, and it was up to all of us to make sure the commands of Allah were strictly obeyed.

My words were accepted by the goat-herders, and they certainly knew of the Sabray cave. They walked past it often and may have seen the armed guard outside. But they uttered not one sentence to the informers. In fact, I gave serious consideration to shooting all four of the Sabray village Taliban supporters but decided instead to bide my time.

Haji Nazer stood guard all day and left only after dark. By then, I'd posted one of my sons at the cave entrance, while I made arrangements for a new evacuation and to establish a different hiding place for Marcus.

It was July 1 now, and in company with another of my sons, plus a village senior man, Norzamund, we made our way back to the cave, crossing the river silently, always alert for activity on the Taliban mountain encampment. This was a quiet night, and we reached Marcus at around midnight.

I have to say, he was very low. I actually thought he'd been crying, and I noticed he'd picked up a piece of flint and scratched some

English words on the rock wall of his Afghan "prison." I had one of my boys copy it down, but I don't think I ever understood what it meant: "God will give me justice."

A few more hours went by before the Sabray team returned and hauled Marcus up for the journey back to the village. It was still very dark—maybe four o'clock—and Marcus realized how badly the Taliban wanted to kill him. But he was just not tuned in to the knife-edge military rules that apply up there. When he flicked on the light of his watch, one of the guards nearly had a heart attack. With his very limited English, the man informed Marcus that if he really wanted to die right now—and get everyone else killed—he'd chosen a very reasonable way to achieve that. The Taliban would spot that pinpoint of light from four hundred yards.

At this stage, the Navy SEAL did not understand the concept of Pashtunwali and all of its ramifications, and certainly not the onerous obligations those ancient tribal laws represented. But he did have to confess disappointment in the efforts of the armed forces to locate him. He had heard US aircrafts overflying the area. But no one seemed anxious to find out what had happened to him.

It was not until he was left in the cave that he began to suspect they'd given up on him. This was his lowest point by far. It was hell's dark in there, and he was all alone, Gulab having failed to mention that he'd been on guard outside all night.

Marcus realized by this time that the village was completely surrounded by the Taliban army he'd fought against two days ago. He did not, however, realize he was responsible for 100 percent of this universal grief to the locals.

He now thought he was finished—that he'd been left to die. He was as near to desperate as he'd ever been, and on top of everything, the plastic bottle he had drank out of had made him sick.

The group reached a flat concrete ground outside a house that would be the American's new temporary home. Gulab and Sarawar proceeded to bring a cot where their guest could rest, while the doctor changed the blood-soaked bandages. Gulab gave Marcus fresh water, which he hoped might cure the black-water fever or whatever it was that had poisoned him.

The American fell asleep instantly. His first visitor showed up around nine o'clock, and attempted to engage him in serious conversation. This proved slightly awkward, since he was only about eight years old and was trying to tell him that he had to become a Muslim like everyone else.

Marcus had no intention of offending him as the boy laid out very seriously the critical words to the prayer that signifies acceptance of the religion of Allah:

La La e La La—Muhammad de la su La La. Marcus was taken with the boy's insistence that he participate in prayer, and he agreed to do it with him.

"At this point, I guess there was some kind of breakthrough," Marcus reflects. "Because he charged out of the room yelling at the top of his lungs for every other kid to join him. When he came back, he was accompanied by about twenty of his buddies—hereinafter, I referred to them as 'my kids.'"

And they were all in the room, jumping up and down and shouting, "Hello, Dr. Marcus! Hello, Dr. Marcus!"

Finally, Gulab showed up and tried unsuccessfully to restore order. He playfully explained to the American that his recitation of the prayer with the little boy meant that he was now a Muslim and would be expected to attend prayers at the village mosque.

- 5 -

SURRENDER THE AMERICAN OR DIE

In the following twenty-four hours, Marcus and Gulab became friends. The Afghani never left his side, and even when other guards were posted on duty inside the house, he remained with him. Gulab, along with the other villagers of Sabray, were embarrassed after the Taliban had broken in and hurt Marcus badly two nights before. It never should have happened, and the fault rested with everyone. The American should not have been left alone in the night hours.

As the senior officer in command, the blame rested on Gulab's shoulders. And he took it to heart, because it had been a military mistake. Sabray was dealing with an army here and the survival of an American battlefield commander.

Two things made it much worse. First, Gulab was working under the direct orders of Allah; and second, he liked this tall Special Forces operator a great deal more than he cared for the rough, sneering gangsters who fought for Ahmad Shah.

That morning, they spent a lot of time trying to communicate with each other. Marcus wanted to know about Gulab's wife and children, and how they were educated up here in the mountains. And while this may have required just a few moments for most people, it took a great deal longer when neither party understood one word the other was saying.

There was, of course, a funny side to it, and the American kept laughing at Gulab's attempts to understand the size of the state of Texas, where his family was from. The Afghani fighter kept trying to ask if it was bigger than one of the local towns, Jalalabad. It took a while for him to grasp that it was bigger than all of Afghanistan.

There is camaraderie between warriors, and they quickly established their humor, and they both laughed easily. For Marcus, this was a huge effort, because he was still in bad pain and actually did not have much to laugh about at all, since they were surrounded by about three hundred hostile, armed tribesmen, every last one of them avowed and determined to shoot the American dead.

Similar to Marcus trying to pass himself off as a doctor, Gulab communicated to Marcus that he was the village policeman. However, Marcus had never thought that Gulab seemed much like a policeman—more like a hardened warrior. But that's what he said, and the SEAL had little choice but to believe him.

Meanwhile, there was serious business to discuss: how they were going to get Marcus away from there. Patrols had been organized around the village. Under Gulab's orders, they were to apprehend any Taliban troops they encountered. They all knew that Shah's men would not dare open fire on the people of Sabray.

A couple of times a day, Gulab rounded up a few armed body-guards, walked over to the Taliban encampment on the mountain, and tried to negotiate. But it was all hopeless.

Shah threatened Gulab, saying repeatedly, "You are going to die. Your wife is going to die, and your children, your little son, all are going to die. Maybe everyone in the village, if you do not hand over the American."

Gulab stared straight into his eyes and told him firmly, "There are many of you, and I know you will kill my family. But I am a muja-hideen commander, and I am not afraid of you. In death, I will take many of you with me. But I will *never* give up the American."

He did not tell Shah that one principal reason was his assessment of what would follow if he were to cave to the terrorist's demand. Everyone would know that Gulab had surrendered, and Shah would tell anyone left alive in Sabray, "Now where is your Lion? We took away your American; General Gulab, he is nothing."

That was a humiliation Gulab could not abide, either in life or in death. For him, there was no decision. The American soldier, he hoped, would fight alongside him if necessary. And he had many rea-sons to believe they would be the finest two warriors on the battle-field.

Gulab was always comforted by the knowledge that Allah likes and approves of prideful men. And He had steered Marcus into the Islamic religion, welcomed him through His children. If they had to fight, they would do so with right on their side. Gulab was sure of that.

Ahmad Shah ended negotiations with a warning: "Mohammed Gulab, if you do not give him up, and the Americans come and bomb us and get him away from here, remember, you will still be in Sabray. We will always know what you have done. We will not forget. You and your family will die."

Gulab glared at him and told him he was surprised he did not understand. "I will not give him up," he said adamantly. "On this earth, I fear only Allah. Certainly not you."

And with that, the Sabray negotiating party returned to the village, leaving the enemy in no doubt that if it made one move, it would face a formidable gunfight from the people. Gulab thinks that deterred the Taliban, who were, after all, still burying their dead.

It also can't be overstated that the Taliban were afraid of Gulab and his older brother Haji Nazer Gul, who was also guarding Marcus. Otherwise they would have stormed into the village again and taken away the American to kill him. But they knew if they tried, many of them would die.

There had been at least two meetings of the village council, and the elders had been certain of their findings: this American had been taken in by the people of Sabray as an act of mercy and in accordance with the teachings and desires of Allah.

The time-honored laws of Pashtunwali made no exceptions. The procedures were sacrosanct. The guest would be defended to the death. No compromise. If the Taliban army attacked, the village would form a line of battle under Gulab's command and defend until no one was left alive; although, hopefully, the Taliban would have retreated long before then.

Either way, there would be no surrender. And everyone understood that, right from the fateful late afternoon of June 29, when Marcus was provided with water, shelter, food, and medical treatment.

From that moment, the village was required to obey the strict first three principles of Pashtunwali: *melmastia* (hospitality), *nanawateh* (protection), and *tureh* (bravery). Complete trust in Allah was inviolate among all Pashtuns.

Gulab thanked Allah at his prayers for the formal support of the people of Sabray, whom very few tribal armies would have dared to fight. From birth, they'd been indoctrinated into the warrior class of these high and remote mountains. The guns of Sabray would match Ahmad Shah's army. Any day.

Nonetheless, Gulab knew it was time for the American to be reacquainted with his own machine gun. He had it brought back to the room that was now his headquarters. After just these few days, Marcus was growing stronger, and Sarawar no longer thought it necessary for him to be under constant medical supervision. His wounds still needed dressing, but not so often.

At this point, Gulab took over as Marcus's permanent guardian until they could summon the Americans to airlift him out of the village. The problem was, this required his guest's cooperation, and there was no way to get him to understand time and distance in these mountains, with their massive gradients and narrow passes. It was a long process.

Working out distance was such a problem that they actually brought in goat-herders from the hills—non-Taliban, of course—to help illustrate the miles and kilometers. And the fact that Marcus operated in some mysterious military measurement he called a "klick" was not helpful.

The goat-herders demonstrated the journey by drawing. But they were short of paper, and the final map had to be scrawled on Marcus's right thigh. In the end, it was not big enough, and they had to switch to his left thigh, a process that almost caused him to jump through the roof with pain.

Gulab remembers how amazed he was that Marcus had somehow traveled seven miles from the battlefield to here, half of it on his hands and knees after he'd been shot. All the tribesmen were shocked that any man could go that far when he was that injured and dying of thirst and blood loss. They must breed very strong doctors in the United States. Gulab, the teak-tough river packhorse, did not think that he could have done it.

Marcus knew there was a small American military outpost two miles away, in a place called Monagee, but it was directly over a towering thousand-foot granite peak, which must have looked like a seven-year hike to Marcus. There was no possibility he could tackle such a journey. At this time, without a man supporting him on either side, he could barely make it outside the front door.

Marcus couldn't communicate well with the villagers, but also, he still did not feel comfortable sharing details of the nearby US outpost. However, they already knew of the larger base in Asadabad and decided that someone would have to go there to inform the Americans that Marcus was safe (more or less). It was somewhere between thirty and forty miles away, depending on the route selected: as ever, steep gradients and winding passes through the mountains are not easy to calculate.

That afternoon, the village elder visited Marcus. He arrived with his usual impeccable manners, bringing the guest tea in the little glass set in its silver holder. He also brought hot, freshly baked bread and some confectionary to be taken with the tea. It was good to see the American eating vigorously—it showed he was getting better.

The elder elected to make the journey on foot by himself, despite his being approximately seventy-five years old. This was principally because he was certain no one would dare to attack him, whereas if younger men were sent, the Taliban might try an ambush.

The most serious point of the discussions involved the swift evacuation of the American, because his enemies out on the mountain were now issuing their threats every couple of hours.

Many people were now being warned that they and their families would die if Gulab would not surrender the Navy SEAL, and while everyone understood that he could not be given up, neither did anyone wish it to be some kind of death sentence hanging over them all. The Pashtuns are known for their long memories, and that most certainly applied also to the gangsters out on the mountain.

In fact, there was already proof that Shah's threats were by no means empty. He meant what he said, and there had been a couple of mysterious deaths inside the village, associates of Gulab's, and they appeared to have been murdered.

Gulab was extremely concerned by this: his own people dying because of his irrevocable pact with God. Marcus, too, had heard the shocking news of the murders, and he tried to make it clear to Gulab that he should be handed over to the Taliban.

Gulab looked at him sternly and told him no, absolutely not. He would not—could not—surrender him, because that would be in defiance of Islam. In truth, though, the American's willingness to make that sacrifice served only to increase Gulab's regard for him.

It was, of course, the ultimate selfless gesture, made by a man he had quickly come to trust. He was as thoroughly brave and decent as Gulab had suspected when the light of Allah first surrounded him.

The village elder conferred with Marcus for more than three hours, slowly and deliberately working out the best route to the US base in Asadabad, and then the correct procedure to follow when he finally arrived there.

There was an enormous level of suspicion between the Pashtun nation and the United States armed forces. They all understood that the arrival of a tribesman from a distant village would likely be greeted with hostility and cynicism. The Americans would probably think he had a bomb strapped to his chest, under his clothes.

Marcus was plainly in no shape to accompany him, so Gulab's brother-in-law would need to travel and negotiate all alone. It was decided that he should carry with him a letter signed by Marcus.

It read: "This man carrying my letter gave me shelter and food, and medical help which saved my life. He is the distinguished village elder in Sabray, and must be believed, and helped at all cost. I am in the care of his family. Signed—Marcus Luttrell."

It was worked out that Maluk would walk at approximately four miles an hour, which meant a nine-hour journey. On that basis, it was decided that he should leave at around nine o'clock at night and, allowing for a one-hour rest break, arrive at the Asadabad base at around seven in the morning, just as the place was awakening. That would give the Americans the daylight hours to mount a rescue.

Walking distances like that are commonplace for the Pashtun, because they have no real roads, and the only form of transportation is a mule cart, which is used for farming and commerce, especially timber. From the earliest age, everyone is accustomed to walking long distances. It's not a hardship. It's just a way of life.

And so, with the strategy planned, the senior men of the village spent much of the evening meeting in Marcus's room and getting to know him better. So far as he was concerned, this was a success. He was one of those people who was easy to befriend, despite the language barrier.

He was wonderful with the children, and the slightly older ones were in and out of his room until they went to bed. They charged back down the hill, yelling, "Hello, Dr. Marcus!"

Discussions in Sabray involved battle positioning if the Taliban attacked. And it became clear that the American would need to stay on the move, because it was vital that Ahmad Shah's men never know his precise location.

Meanwhile, Gulab took an armed patrol out every two hours and walked right through the village, checking houses, gardens, and hiding places. Occasionally they saw furtive movement, but the Taliban had no wish to end up in a firefight in a group of houses that afforded Gulab's men shelter but granted nowhere for them to take cover.

None of the Taliban stayed, and they scuttled away up the mountain back to their encampment. Gulab had made it clear to Shah that if there were any attack, or even trespass on Sabray, they would be shot on sight.

No one, however, has ever accused Shah of being anything but a bold commander, and late that night Gulab was walking between houses when he heard the unmistakable sound of strangers creeping around. These were not villagers. They were outsiders.

Gulab slammed his rifle into firing position against his shoulder and challenged the intruders. There followed the sound of running feet.

Needless to say, Gulab was not afraid, and neither were the men who accompanied him. But the warning was stark and obvious. These tribesmen from off the mountain were out looking for Marcus, trying to pinpoint the house he was in.

And they may have discovered something, which meant that the American had to be moved before they returned with a bigger, more powerful force. Gulab posted guards and took one man with him back to the house to collect Marcus and blankets.

Swiftly they gathered their equipment and assisted the wounded American in getting up and out of there. They grabbed his arms and held them across their shoulders. He was still a big weight, but he tried to walk, and he was half-carried out of the house. They grabbed his rifle and a magazine, and brought those as well.

It was a slow, quiet process before they made a left turn and stepped up and onto the roof of a different house. The occupants knew they were up there, Gulab having cleared this fallback position earlier in the evening. But it was so dark, they could see nothing— not five yards in front of their faces.

For all Gulab knew, there were half a dozen Taliban killers waiting in the night, right below the roof.

But it was difficult for Marcus, and it took many minutes to lower him onto the roof and get him covered up without a lot of scuffling. He tried to speak once, and Gulab says he reacted as if he'd just fired a pistol.

"*Sssshhhhh!* Dr. Marcus," he hissed, "Taliban hear you, they try to kill us!"

He did, of course, realize that Marcus could not understand one word of his warning, but the American picked up on the urgency in Gulab's voice and did not speak again. The two Afghanis lay down on either side of him, very close together for warmth, each with a blanket. It was painfully uncomfortable on the rock-hard mud-brick mattress, but Marcus was disciplined. He never moved, never spoke.

Gulab thought then, not for the first time, that this man was a highly trained warrior. That was clear on the night the Taliban broke into his room, when he kept telling them he was only a doctor on duty in the mountains to tend the American wounded. But, says Gulab, "If Marcus was a doctor, I'm a nursemaid."

Hour after hour, they lay there motionless, each with a light grip on a combat rifle. Across the dark roofs, they could occasionally see lights moving on the hillside, but no sounds came from the street below. The interlopers had been scared off earlier in the evening by the sudden snap of the magazine in Gulab's AK.

And when the sun finally climbed above the eastern peaks of the Hindu Kush, there were no more intruders. The guards left Marcus for a few minutes to check that all was quiet, and then went back for him and helped him back to the house. But it was no longer safe to leave him alone for even a couple of minutes, since no one knew how closely the village was being watched by the Taliban troops.

This meant that personal prayers each morning had to be conducted inside the house. They all believed it was dangerous to leave the American alone, and everyone felt the obligation Allah had bestowed upon Gulab. Thus, for that entire week, prayers were said in Marcus's room.

Everyone prayed for him. They prayed for his safe deliverance from the evil of the Taliban and for his wounds to heal. Above all, they prayed for a safe journey for Maluk, the fearless village elder, on his hazardous journey across the hills to get help.

Against the call to prayers was the noisy testimony of about twenty of the village children. The noise was ridiculous, in this temporary mosque, and they could all see Marcus laughing at the kids. Also, the tribesmen knew when they were beaten. Daily prayers would from now on be held right here with Marcus, and prayers would be offered for him until he was safe.

134

And it seemed that Marcus, too, was happy to comply. When he prayed with Gulab and his protectors, he rose from his cot and used a prayer mat. Of course, only he knew to whom he prayed, but to those around him, he was in the care of, and at the mercy of, Allah, and that's how he behaved, respectfully and piously.

That morning after the night on the roof, the temporary mosque was less peaceful than normal, owing to an intense overfly of US warplanes. At first, Marcus seemed unconcerned, but several of them were flying over and then turning right around and coming back, throttling down their engines, as if searching for something.

Marcus plainly thought they were searching for him or for his colleagues, and at the end of prayers, he rushed outside as fast as his battered left leg would carry him. He ripped off his shirt and stood in the street waving it high above his head, shouting at the top of his lungs to the US pilots above.

It all came to nothing as they just flew away, back to the west, and Gulab could see the terrible disappointment in Marcus's face. "I could tell," he said, "Marcus felt they'd just given up on him."

The sudden dash outside to try to attract attention might have had a drastic effect. Gulab could see that he was in terrible pain whenever he tried to move. His shoulder was by now a major problem, and he could barely lift his right arm. His back was killing him because it was so hard for him to stand. It required only one glance at his left thigh to imagine the agonizing pain.

Gulab's solution was an ancient tribal remedy, tobacco opium, and he sent for an old village resident to bring some to the house.

Marcus was a bit skeptical at the sight of this greenish-looking compound, which resembles bread dough mixed with grass.

But he was in such pain, he'd have tried anything, and he ripped off a chunk and placed it between his inner lip and his teeth. Gulab knew it would work very fast, and he just sat there with him until Marcus began to smile. Opium was the best possible antidote for pain, and he could almost see the agony of his wounds drain out of Marcus. When Gulab asked him if he felt better, Marcus replied, *"Hooyah,* Gulab!"

Not easily translatable, but anyone could see he was so much better. Gulab tried to explain what the opium plant was, and how they were able to grow it up here in the mountains, and how it was their most profitable crop, as well as their principal medical solution to violent pain.

With hand signals, Gulab pointed out the flat below the village, where the opium was grown. It is likely that Marcus had already noticed that this walled-in empty plateau—a couple of acres, though hard up against the mountain wall, and with a steep drop on its southern side—was the only area in the vicinity flat enough for a rescue helicopter to land.

Marcus's whole mood changed once his pain had eased, and he was able to eat some hot flat bread. He even tried some of the goat's milk. But not much, preferring to stick with fresh water. Gulab handed the whole bag of opium to Marcus, in case he was there for several more days.

No one had heard yet whether Maluk had made it to the American base, but throughout the day, there was persistent activity in the sky as US aircraft swept over the village. In Gulab's view, the elder had reached the base and informed them they had Marcus safe.

The US aircraft were almost certainly conducting a recce—reconnaissance—as they were certainly aware of the hostile Taliban encampment right there on the mountain. He was no expert on American air power, but Gulab did recognize the MH-47 Chinooks, accompanied by several sinister-looking Sikorsky Black Hawk UH-60 gunships.

None of Shah's men opened fire from the mountain, which was probably wise. Those modern Black Hawks were many times more lethal than the Russian helos that the mujahideen had downed. A Black Hawk 60 is equipped with machine guns, rockets, and laser-guided missiles. Just one of them could inflict heavy damage.

Marcus continued to spot his American aircraft overflying the village, yet he received no sign or signal that they still intended to rescue him. It was hard to take. He constantly tried to imagine himself in their shoes—not having heard a word from anyone since Mikey made the fatal last call on his cell phone. They might well have assumed that everyone was dead, but that was unlikely. SEALs never admit to a team member's death until they've seen the body. However, Mikey had said they were dying, which must have at least alerted someone that either one or two Redwings was possibly still alive but probably injured.

And that would have triggered a whole new set of problems, because there was almost nowhere a helo could put down on these massive gradients without toppling over. Marcus now understood there was the opium field, but that was about it. And those flat pastures were hell's close to the mountain wall, and very exposed to Taliban gunfire and rockets.

He kept thinking of the small, upright figure of the village elder, striding through the passes with his long walking staff. He should have been at the US base by now, God willing. All hopes now rested upon Maluk, Sabray's brave and distinguished tribal leader.

But it was his brother-in-law, Mohammed Gulab, who was the most important figure in Marcus's life. He had personally organized the security, made certain there was always water and food, and he had provided the substance which so dramatically eased the pain. Marcus had nearly lost count of the times that Gulab faced the Taliban leaders, growling at them that the big Texan would not be handed over. Gulab had gone out on the mountain and told them what would happen if they dared to attack. And now Gulab came to him again, this time to reveal a new letter he'd received—not from Ahmad Shah but from his firebrand of a deputy, "Commodore" Abdul. (Why the Afghani fighter had assumed a British Royal Navy rank six thousand feet above sea level was beyond Marcus.) Abdul had a growing reputation as an ambush expert and a highly trained killer, and now he was making a formal demand that the villagers of Sabray hand over the American immediately. Gulab took a while to show Marcus that. He and Maluk had already sent a reply to the "Commodore," which stated that they did not care how desperately the Taliban wanted their guest, they were not going to get him, and that was an end to it.

Gulab let Marcus know, by signs and angry facial expressions, that the Taliban could not frighten him, no matter what they did or said. He also suggested they needed Sabray a lot more than Sabray needed them.

By this time, the American was filled with admiration for this Gulab character, who was a confident, courageous man, a natural leader, and of a somewhat more decisive turn of mind than a village cop. Marcus had every reason to trust him as much as he'd ever trusted any man, but there was something exceptional about Gulab, something distinctive.

If they'd shared a language, they'd have become immediate friends. They laughed at the same things, and Gulab looked grave when he suspected danger, and he quite willingly tried to tell Marcus everything about his life and family, albeit with only limited success. Also, there were tribal taboos that no Afghan will ever reveal, yet Gulab did his best to explain them to the American.

In retrospect, he was obviously a leading force in the village. Gulab's requests, and certainly his orders, were obeyed instantly by anyone he addressed. Marcus knew nothing of the former mujahideen commander, or the boy machine gunner; certainly nothing of the Lion of Sabray. All this came much later. Nevertheless, he did understand that he was in the hands of an extremely significant person, who was palpably not intimidated by Ahmad Shah or his "Commodore" sidekick.

Not intimidated does not mean careless. Gulab never took a chance if there was any indication the Taliban were coming in after his guest. He reacted calmly and defensively—a lot like a man used to deploying troops.

Gulab's other unmissable quality was a complete disinterest in money or a reward of any kind. Marcus's own gratitude to him was overwhelming, since he could, after all, have left him to die on the riverbank and saved everyone a lot of trouble.

He tried to give him the excellent watch, which at the time represented a fair proportion of Marcus's worldly goods. But Gulab would not hear of it, even though it was offered several times. He spoke quickly in his own dialect and somehow imparted that he wished only to do the will of Allah.

To accept any kind of compensation would not be in accordance with Pashtunwali. Gulab's goodness was of a higher calling, and Marcus eventually understood that, language-strapped as he plainly was.

Friendship is an elusive principle—in some cases, perhaps the most powerful binding force there is. It's that way between many SEALs. But the Texan sensed it with Gulab. They'd forged a bond based on trust, which might last a lifetime. Such profound friendships may well be exclusive to fighting men, who have faced down death together, as these two most certainly had. And were still doing.

The morning passed slowly, and since there did seem to be some aerial activity, Marcus rigged up his radio emergency beacon and jammed it in the window, aiming skyward. He hoped that the batteries were still sufficiently strong to transmit the beam that would alert the US pilots to the glad news that he was still alive. Of course, he knew the main risk: that the guys would assume the beacon had been stolen by the Taliban and was now being activated to tempt US pilots down to low altitude in the area.

From their secret bunkers and caves, the tribesmen could unleash Stingers and try to down the aircraft. At this time, Marcus still did not know exactly what they had pulled off four nights ago, when they blew up the rescue helo coming to get the Redwings out of there.

He did, however, know that their favorite trick was to slam their missiles in through the open ramp of the helos, and blast the fuel tanks. This was a tactic at which they were skilled enough to frighten the bejesus out of any US pilot flying too low and too slow in search of a lost SEAL.

If the Taliban nurtured those kinds of ambitions on this morning of July 2, however, they were badly out of luck. The village elder must have reached Asadabad, because suddenly all hell broke loose on the mountains. In came the US fighter bombers, which literally bombarded the slopes upon which the Taliban camp was situated.

Marcus heard the bombs come in: big 1,200-pounders slamming into the granite, blowing apart huge rocks, knocking down trees, and generally rearranging the landscape. They were so tight on their targets, they nearly blasted the village of Sabray off the mountain. Roofs went flying into the air, parts of house walls caved in, there was dust everywhere, kids were crying, women screaming. Gulab and Marcus were crouched against the walls, inside, heads well down, awaiting the departure of the US planes.

As suddenly as it had started, the bombardment ceased. The US planes had not hit the village with a direct shot, but the peripheral damage was unavoidable. Doubtless it had softened up the Taliban and caused them endless casualties, as the Americans had definitely intended. But it also must have left them spitting with anger, and it was obvious that Gulab believed a sustained personal attack was imminent.

The people of Sabray, however, seemed to hold nothing against the Americans. They set to work, every man, woman, and child, clearing up the mess, replacing stones, fixing roofs and doors, trying to make their dwellings waterproof. By nightfall, they had restored order.

Soon after the evening meal, when the young kids had gone to bed, the most unimaginable electrical storm ripped through these mountains. Texans are no strangers to hurricanes and twisters back home, but it was a rainstorm the likes of which Marcus had never seen in his life. Great jagged bolts of lightning slashed across the sky, accompanied by gigantic claps of thunder, and the rain hammered against the escarpments and then cascaded down any downward route there was: gullies, cart tracks, dried-up riverbeds. The torrent that gushed through the middle of Sabray would have swept any living creature off the face of the mountain.

Outside the front door, the dirt-track road had been turned into a river, and the noise was deafening. The upper pathway down to the village was a waterfall. The whole sky above the high peaks was a weird electric blue. It looked like a prelude to the end of the world.

Gulab and Marcus sat with their backs to the thick rock wall constructed against the mountain. They'd suffered no damage in the US bombardment, and the building remained waterproof. Nothing leaked, and they weren't swept away. But the rain belted down nonstop for six hours until 0300 in the morning. Because of the steep gradient, the floodwater went away fairly quickly, gushing down the mountain. In less than an hour, it had cleared.

Marcus had been harboring an unlikely plan that he would somehow walk over the Afghan Alps "like one of Hannibal's friggin' elephants," and make it to the small US base at Monagee. But now conditions on the saturated mountain would plainly be treacherous, making such a journey out of the question. Also, he'd slept for many hours since midnight, and Gulab had decided against waking him.

So he had nothing to do except sit and contemplate the impossible while feeling sicker and sicker by the hour. Parasites in the water plus his weakened immune system were draining him. Marcus eventually took another dose of opium and knocked himself back out.

He didn't wake up until the sun was high in the sky. He was frustrated at the world. He desperately wanted out of the village and at least wanted word that his people knew he was there and alive. He didn't know for certain whether the elder had made it through. Everything hurt like hell, and less than a half mile away sat Ahmad Shah and the "Commodore," trying to dream up ways to kill him right here, or, alternately, drag him over the border to Pakistan and decapitate him.

Marcus also could see that Gulab was worried about possible Taliban retaliation for the US attack the previous day. His friend was pacing and looking out the window. He'd also posted guards on the periphery of the village.

So as not to let Gulab's mood completely unnerve him, Marcus took a walk around the village. Suddenly there was a near-frantic rush of footsteps behind him as Gulab came racing down the mountainside, calling loudly, "Marcus! Marcus! Run! Taliban are here!"

He almost dragged the SEAL. Marcus could tell this was urgent, and did everything he could to move faster. But he'd forgotten his rifle, and he pulled back to tell him of this omission. Gulab, who was clutching his own AK, looked at the American as if he'd finally lost his mind. But he kept going, dragging Marcus behind him, just the two of them, floundering toward the lower reaches of the village. It was unclear whether they were going straight through and then over the river to the secret cave, or whether they would make a stand in one of the strong stone houses on the lowest dirt street—hopefully one with some narrow windows, firing areas, from where they could cut down the enemy.

Behind them, among the higher buildings in the village, they heard intermittent gunfire—the sounds of troops firing randomly into the air. Marcus remembers stumbling down this steep hill. *Jesus!* he thought to himself. *This could be Murphy's Ridge all over again, and here I am with two full magazines in my gun harness and nothing to fire 'em with.*

Gulab admits that it was a bitter disappointment to learn that Marcus had left his rifle behind, because the Talban might find it and take reprisals against the owners of the house where he had sought shelter. And then there was the reality that Gulab needed him to shoot before the Taliban destroyed them both.

But at that moment, his prime objective was to find cover, from where they could regroup, get organized, and make a stand. It was essential they get into a military-style redoubt before the Taliban had even a remote idea where they were.

Gulab remembers that race down the mountain, because it was there that he understood once and for all that Marcus, a highly trained member of the US Special Forces, had enough strength to move on his own and demonstrate his training as an elite soldier. Every loose gunshot they heard, he instinctively ducked down low to the ground yet still kept running. And each time Gulab turned to tell Marcus "Get down! Crouch! Run low!" he was already in position a split second before the Afghani.

They reached the lowest level in the village and rushed into a house owned by a friend. It was perfectly situated, with excellent views up the hill into the main residential area. Its walls were thick, with a couple of windows on the front facing the street.

Gulab helped Marcus sit down in a dark corner, virtually out of sight, and then he took off out of the house, running hard, back up into the area where the Taliban troops were still firing erratically into the air.

He dodged through houses, through backyards, around the mosque. He skipped across the main street, skirted carefully past the adjacent homes, and lunged through the window of the house where Marcus had recuperated. Almost without breaking stride, he grabbed the Navy SEAL's rifle, tucked a spare ammunition clip into his pocket, clambered back out the window, and then charged back down the mountain, this time using the outer pathway on the right flank, as the Taliban had drifted to the center, and appeared to be in some kind of conference.

No one saw him, and he half ran, half stumbled back down the steep slope, the way he had as a kid and the way his forefathers had done before him. He hit the door with his shoulder, handed Marcus his rifle, and told him gravely, "Taliban, Marcus. We fight."

Right there began the transformation from injured American into battle-commander Marcus. He climbed to his feet and stared around the room, looking for a big, heavy chest of drawers that they could heave in front of the door and jam into position. Unhappily, there was nothing, just those huge, colored Afghan cushions. So they shoved them into place right in front of the door. Anything to slow down a forward rush into the room by a heavily armed enemy.

That was when Marcus took over. The SEAL team leader rammed a magazine into his Mark 12 with deft expertise. Then he demonstrated his own defensive position in the left-hand window, standing crouched in the corner, with the rifle sights aimed up the hill.

Marcus then moved Gulab back, to the right, and showed him how he wanted him to fire from that window, but to be ever ready to step back, swivel left, and fire straight at the back door, blasting apart anyone who shoved his way in and tried to shoot him in the back.

He checked Gulab's magazine, checked his own, and then announced a readiness to "rock 'n' roll."

Two men against maybe fifty, but the American soldier acted throughout as if they would beat them. Gulab could tell that Marcus thought they'd turn them back.

The houses in lower Sabray were quite close, and if one or more Taliban tried to come down the circuitous path through the village, they would have to pop out between buildings, right in front of their eyes.

They checked the cushions in front of the door and jammed themselves in the window frames, machine guns ready, classic infantry defensive positions, awaiting an offensive move from the enemy. They could hear the raiders high above these lower streets, and now they both heard a barrage of shooting and wondered whether there was an exchange of fire between the Taliban and the villagers.

Since both sides used the Russian Kalashnikov, Gulab couldn't tell from listening who was shooting what. However, he knew there were several armed men behind the walls of many village houses, ready to open fire, in ruthless defense of the American guest.

Marcus and Gulab were in warrior stance gazing up the hill. Any member of the Taliban force heading directly to this house, down either route, would inevitably die. The Afghan-US team was locked in, and locked on, firing from behind solid, stone walls; both expert, trained firefighters.

And there was an air of confidence about Marcus. It was as if Gulab was seeing him in his true environment at last, and this was an awesome sight, one huge US Special Forces commander, primed for action, well positioned, and spoiling for a battle. And for almost a half hour, it seemed that he would get his wish. The gunfire increased high above them, but it sounded very random—not the controlled aim-and-fire of highly trained troops. Gulab guessed that the Taliban troops had simply rushed out of the woods and begun a short campaign to terrify the women and children of Sabray—and grab or shoot Marcus if they could.

The two of them stayed in position for another fifteen minutes, and then, quite suddenly, the gunfire died away, and there was silence save for the normal sounds of village life. Gulab knew that Ahmad Shah's thugs had left, but out of caution, the pair remained in position for another half hour.

As two military officers, ordinarily Marcus and Gulab would each seek a debrief, but, of course, neither could speak to the other. But they were both thinking the same thing: someone had tipped off the Taliban about where Marcus was being sheltered, and Shah had decided on a swift strike. When charging into the house failed, they retreated, perhaps not wishing to encounter controlled gunfire from the Navy SEAL and the mujahideen commander, for not many nights had passed since the Taliban had suffered a baptism of fire from a four-man American insertion team.

This left the home team feeling more optimistic, but when they finally emerged from the temporary redoubt, they proceeded very cautiously, as if unseen eyes on the far hillside were watching through stolen Russian glasses. Also, they could not be certain that Ahmad Shah had not posted marksmen on the outskirts of the village—men who just might gun them down if they attempted to get back to the house.

For this reason, Gulab elected not to go back up but instead to make their way farther down the mountain, *away* from the village, and wait to see what developed. It was his firm view that Maluk had made it to Asadabad, and that the Americans were now well briefed, and were preparing to come in and get their man.

So once more they set off down the slope, and again Gulab could see that Marcus was in terrible pain. One of his men had joined them and helped him down, with the Texan's huge arms wrapped around their shoulders.

They reached the opium field and rested for a bit. The SEAL was staring at this unique piece of flat ground, contemplating what they all knew: that if the US rescue team landed, it would do so right here on the one piece of flat ground in the entire area.

None of them wanted to go too far away, and they made their way up into the hillsides, where the vegetation was thickest and where most of the rays of the hot sun could not penetrate.

Marcus found a soft spot under some kind of a bush and discovered a crop of blackberries growing all around him. He just lay there on his back, eating them voraciously. He was trying to relax, despite the fact that they were almost surrounded by Taliban troops ready to shoot him dead if they got half a chance. Without getting their heads blown off by Gulab, that is.

The three of them sat there for a while, but there were infinitesimal sounds in the trees, deep in this woodland territory—the slightest snap of a distant twig; an unnatural swish of a high branch; movement in the still, windless grasses and ferns—where there should have been none.

Gulab considered the Taliban were closing in on them, and he whispered to Marcus in Pashtun, "We must go now." Somehow the

American understood, and he reached for his rifle and turned over. But he hesitated and for some reason turned around and stared up the hill. And there, sitting on a rock, staring down at them, was Ahmad Shah.

They both knew precisely who he was, and for a moment, Gulab froze. Marcus instantly leveled his rifle into firing position, and he had it aimed straight for Shah's forehead. He was very obviously giving serious consideration to pulling the trigger, which, from where Gulab sat, was a rather short-sighted plan.

Shah was surrounded by his army, and their boss was being threatened by the wounded American they had been seeking for four days. They were leaning forward now, more visible in their trees, with even more Taliban infantry moving up into the area.

Marcus and Shah stared at each other. The terrorist chief knew he was essentially a dead man if any one of his men opened fire. Either Marcus or Gulab would blow him away, but in the ensuing minutes, the Taliban would probably mow down both of them—and probably the entire village—furious at having lost their beloved leader.

So there they were in a tense Mexican standoff. Within seconds, they all knew that no one was in much of a position to shoot anyone without causing untold damage. Ahmad Shah lowered his rifle and, looking directly at Marcus, gave an almost imperceptible nod of his head.

That was a signal for a brief conference. Gulab finally stood up, nodded back at him, and then set off up the hill, walking, he knew, into the teeth of very great danger. Because now they could shoot him and then shoot Marcus, one at a time. If nothing else, that would avoid the kind of massacre that would end any goodwill the Taliban still had from the people of Sabray.

Ahmad Shah was identical to the image in the grainy photograph issued to the Redwings by the SEAL ops room: a glowering, hate-filled fanatic, with wisps of red in his beard—an Afghan bent on destroying the US occupying force and his own Kabul government, more or less in that order.

Marcus stared right at him, straight down the barrel of his trusty Mark 12, and gave serious thought to pressing the trigger and taking him out. But SEALs are not cowboys. They don't shoot from the hip, at least not regularly, and Marcus weighed the consequences. If he shot him, Gulab would immediately hit the dirt and shoot as many Taliban as possible. But there were dozens of them in the trees, and in the end, they'd win, what with Gulab and Marcus being trapped on open ground on a downslope. And then, contemplating the loss of their beloved leader, they'd surely march into Sabray and take out the entire population in their anger and disappointment.

The American decided not to shoot, but he never took his eyes off Shah or lowered the rifle. In fairness, Marcus will confirm that his adversary never flinched; he just kept right on staring back with that look of absolute hatred on his face.

Suddenly Shah turned to Gulab, and what passed between them can only be guessed, but it was probably a lot more hatred. Marcus stayed right where he was, the Mark 12 trained on Shah's head. And then he saw Gulab stand up, his head held high, and walk out toward Shah, right under the gunsights of the enemy.

He thought then, as he thinks now, that Gulab displayed a very rare act of gallantry. It reminded him of Mikey, and, in a way, it was equally moving. Marcus had been on his own in this strange place, thousands of miles from home, with so many people wishing him dead, and there walked this man who had saved his life and had stood powerfully between the SEAL and his sworn enemies.

He was a still a man to whom he could not speak, but who had cared for him as if he were his own brother. He was, by any standard, Marcus's beloved savior. And now once more he walked into the jaws of death for the wounded American.

Marcus watched Gulab and Shah walk away, out of sight, into the mountain forest. He didn't really know if he would ever see his new friend again. And he knew that if this should be so, he had, at most, minutes to live. Because if they shot Gulab, they'd surely execute their real target.

The tribesman from Sabray left Marcus behind and walked along-side this self-appointed general, head of his own army, and flanked by his self-appointed "Commodore" deputy. They stepped several paces into the trees, leaving Marcus all alone, under the guns of the Taliban marksmen.

They stepped into a small clearing, and Ahmad Shah handed Gulab a piece of paper on which were written these words, in Pash-tun: "Either you hand over the American, or every member of your family will be killed."

Gulab read this carefully and placed the paper in his pocket. He stared at this so-called warrior-savior of Afghanistan, and he told himself, *This character is not a recognized head of a national army; he's not even approved by the government. He's a usurper, a man seeking power for himself at whatever cost.*

So he glared straight into his eyes. "Ahmad Shah," said Gulab, "neither I nor my people will ever give up the American. And *we* function under the ancient laws of our people, and I, under the direct command of Allah.

"I am surprised you cannot understand that. But should you decide to defy those ancient laws or the commands of Allah, I must advise you that the consequences for you may be very serious and may last until the end of your days. I cannot stop you and all these troops you have from killing me and my family, and perhaps everyone else in Sabray.

"And I am not suggesting you will face the fires of hell. Only Allah can do that. But I am His devout servant, and He has spoken to me, and I know that God is great, and there is but one God.

"And I say to you, to hell with your threats. I will never be afraid of you. I am Gulab, the Lion of Sabray, and I stand alongside the one and only God in my belief that the American must be protected."

Gulab turned his back on him and began walking back through the trees to Marcus. Shah called out to him, reminding that he lived only because he, Shah, allowed that to be so. Gulab gripped his rifle and told the Taliban commander that *he* lived only because, he, Gulab, permitted it.

Gulab walked back to Marcus. All around, he could see the men of Sabray, who had somehow heard of this confrontation and then swarmed down the hill, armed to the teeth, toward the American's blackberry bush. These were trained warriors—mujahideen veterans and younger men—many of them taught by Gulab. They understood lines of battle and had positioned themselves in trees as well as behind bushes and rocks. This tight, practiced formation would be more than a match for Shah's force.

And they had the added advantage of knowing every inch of this ground. If someone moved a rock beside a trail by a matter of a few feet, they would know because they had probably seen it all of their lives.

Gulab's judgment was that Shah would order his men to hold their fire. Yes, there would be other opportunities for him to murder the village's premier warrior and his family, but not today—not while Gulab had the mass protection of the Sabray fighters.

The last thing the Taliban troops needed was another bloodbath. In Gulab's view, Ahmad Shah was already playing with fire. In the past week, he had lost many, many men to American gunfire and a US air bombardment on the mountain.

Troops can take only so much of a battering without their morale collapsing, and it would have been amazing if these hidden gunmen had decided to start shooting.

Praise be to Allah, they did not. Gulab walked back to Marcus, who, unsurprisingly, was extremely anxious to know what had happened. He showed the Navy SEAL the piece of paper and in sign language explained to him what it said.

Gazing around them, they could see the Taliban dispersing back to the encampment on the mountain overlooking the village—or, at least, what remained of that encampment, after the American bombers had finished with it.

There was no doubt in Gulab's mind that Shah and his men would be back and would never give up on their quest to kill Marcus. But that did not mean they would be successful. Nevertheless, Gulab elected not to return to the house where they had taken shelter.

He leaned down, took Marcus by the hand, and helped haul him to his feet. It was very obvious that the American's shattered left leg was giving him huge pain, and he'd left the opium in the house. But two more of Gulab's men arrived to help lift him to higher ground in order to find a new place of safety. It was an arduous walk until they reached a dried-up riverbed and set the agonized Marcus down in a comfortable position. Someone produced water.

They stayed there for forty-five minutes. All around them, keeping a fifty-yard distance, were Gulab's friends—familiar faces to Marcus—every one of them armed. Some were positioned in the trees, some at ground level, all ready to open fire with a mass assault on the Taliban if the enemy threatened.

For the moment, that threat was gone. They were safe temporarily. But Gulab remembers being a lot less confident than he appeared. And he racked his brain for a new plan; somewhere different to hide the wounded American warrior.

Gulab was faced with a hard decision. He had to get Marcus away from Ahmad Shah and the Commodore; somewhere secret where they would not find him. For all anyone knew, they were being spied upon at this very moment as they trekked painfully uphill into the hidden woodlands of the Hindu Kush.

They also could not stray very far from Sabray, because Marcus required food, medical supplies, and fresh water. The logical place was back in the cold, dark cave.

The senior tribesman had a vague plan and a vague idea of the territory to which they were headed. But nothing definite.

They just kept moving up the footpath, which was so slippery and muddy, it was a miracle Marcus did not keel over and collapse on the ground. Two friends were bearing much of his weight, but Marcus is a very big man, and the gradient was steep. They were virtually pushing 230 pounds uphill.

Gulab's hopes were now pinned on the Americans, but if they were going to thunder in out of the skies and save Marcus, they should have been there two nights ago. If Maluk had made it to Asadabad, where were they? By now, they must have had the letter Marcus wrote for the elder to carry with him, and surely the US military would have come instantly to gather up its injured hero.

But no one had heard anything. The US bombardment of the mountainside had seemed so promising, but after that, only silence. Like four little lost goats, they inched their way up through the still-dripping trees, slipping, sliding, and heaving. Marcus endured the worst of it, but he battled upward without a word of complaint, although anyone could see he was in the most terrible pain.

- 6 -

"IT'S MARCUS, GUYS! WE GOT HIM!"

It has remained forever a mystery to Gulab why Marcus's rescuers took so long. But years later, he can now be informed. Backtracking several days, gaps can be filled because information has only now been declassified.

When the message that a big Bagram-based Chinook was down in the mountains in a failed attempt to rescue a four-man SEAL team flashed through to the forward operating bases (FOB) in the Hindu Kush close to the border with Pakistan, it caused instant consternation. Everyone knew it included Marcus, Axe, and Danny. According to the last comms, at least two of the four were dead. It was assumed there were no survivors from the helo.

This was a five-alarm uproar, shaping up as the worst day in US

Special Forces history. And immediately, the US Army Rangers and the Green Berets began volunteering for a new rescue mission. People were demanding that a helo get fired up right away, since dozens of these professional hard men were preparing to ride in like the "friggin' Seventh Cavalry."

This, however, was less than straightforward, since Sabray had no road and nothing even remotely resembling an airstrip. Militarily, it was unapproachable, except on foot. And this put the commanding officer of CJSOTF (Combined Joint Special Operations Task Force—either Rangers or Green Berets, or a combination) into a major dilemma.

The issue was knife-edged. And the question for the CO was fraught with tension: Do I risk my only air transport up here in the badlands for the possibility of rescuing perhaps one man, in the full knowledge that the Taliban are experts with Stinger missiles?

The officer's answer was a very reluctant no. But, not for the first time, the Green Berets had swarmed into action, anyway. While CJSOTF was wrestling with the problem, the Green Berets were already in a helicopter flying from Jalalabad to Asadabad, where they demanded major transport up to Sabray, with the sole objective of "kicking some serious Taliban ass and getting the SEALs home, quick."

There were already problems everywhere, not the least because of the shocking terrain. No vehicle was capable of crossing the steep mountain to get anywhere near Sabray. Plus, the weather was closing in, there were thunderstorms in the area, and the ground was already soaked, treacherous, and, in places, impassable.

"Mission impossible" was the planners' verdict. And no one was anxious to take another $35 million helicopter loss until they at least had a definite objective—for instance, an American had been confirmed alive and in need of rescue.

They call it POSIDENT.

The high command was not saying "no" unreasonably. Every shred of logic was telling them that it was a risk too far to order dozens of top men to try to walk and climb over the mountain range, probably under Taliban guns. To many people, this was an obvious nonstarter. And strictly on paper, it probably was.

But a Green Beret major to whom Marcus will forever be grateful answered, "Sir, the guys are determined to go. If we have to walk, we'll walk."

"It's twenty miles to the village," was the reply. "It's across hostile Taliban country. Ground conditions are awful. You'll have no vehicles; certainly no heavy weapons. And it'll soon be dark. Those twenty miles over that terrain are gonna feel like five hundred."

"I'm not sure you quite understand, sir," replied the major. "We're not leaving them."

No one was ever told the blow-by-blow discussions that followed that declaration, but they virtually hijacked a dozen big trucks from the adjoining US Marine base, aided and abetted by a couple of sympathetic senior marine officers who also would not hear of the SEALs being abandoned.

They made one stipulation: "Gas up the trucks, but you have to take one marine with each one. This is strictly against regulations, but it'll be a darned sight worse if we don't even have guys with the vehicles!" Semper fidelis, right?

Also on the Asadabad base were a few other SEALs, from Team Ten, Team Six, and a separate squadron of Rangers. Every last one insisted on joining the rescue party. Then they heard that another platoon of Rangers had done the same thing at their base on the other side of the mountain and were treating the operation like it was the Normandy invasion in 1944. The Rangers were prepared to do anything to try to save Mikey, Danny, Axe, and Marcus.

The result was that 120 members of the United States Special Forces—Green Berets and Army Rangers—clad in heavy-duty waterproofs, carrying climbing gear, compasses, medical supplies, food, and a ton of ammunition, set off that afternoon for Sabray. The Green Berets drove out of the base in convoy in the marine trucks; the Rangers, from the other start point, were on foot.

They all had a highly dangerous journey ahead of them, and they headed into the mountains, up the first escarpments, under low cloud cover. The marine trucks made short work of the first few miles, lurching and growling their way up the gradients, but the two dozen Rangers had a tough time—especially when the night turned pitch-black. Nonetheless, they kept going with short rests, making only a snail's pace across the rocky face of Afghanistan's northeastern range.

All too swiftly, of course, the Green Berets ran out of road. They came to a halt at the head of a valley and circled the wagons, making doubly sure that the Taliban could not follow them in there. The marines left a guard detail to protect the vehicles and seal off the entire valley.

There followed several conferences in which the Green Beret leaders, who are apt to be even more headstrong than their counterparts in the SEALs, swore to God they were the mountain men of the US Army, deeply experienced, experts on the gradients, unstoppable in battle, and the best climbers this side of Mount Everest's north face.

Probably true—nearly as good as the SEALs. At this point, another of Marcus's great buddies, Staff Sergeant Travis (twenty-seven then, and still serving now), was calling a lot of the shots. He instructed one of the native troops—the locals who usually accompany Special Forces in Afghanistan—to scout around a few local villages and see if he could round up some transport: horses, yaks, oxen, whatever.

The kid came back with about fifty donkeys. Then he went back out and returned with another twenty. The guys spent hours loading them with all the equipment out of the trucks. There were piles of rucksacks, all their food and water, medical supplies, plus a few heavy machine guns, ammunition, mortar tubes, and God knows what else.

Thus, when they finally set off, they looked like a mobile army trying to take over a country: 120 armed troops, seventy fully laden donkeys, trotting along the line astern, roped together, braying through the long, echoing mountain passes on their seven-mile journey to Sabray.

High above, the Green Beret commanders had called in air cover:

occasional Apache helicopters swooping in and then returning to base; A-10 Thunderbolt IIs riding shotgun; and a Lockheed AC-130 Spectre gunship, all ready to dive through the mountains and into the fray should the Taliban army become ambitious.

As Travis said years later, "A lot of people said we looked just like Brigadier General Frank Merrill's guys: a rough, unkempt, armed mule train, hacking our way across the face of the mountain, ready for anything." One way or another, Staff Sergeant Travis and his boys looked like a twenty-first-century version of Merrill's Marauders: the epic American special jungle warfare force that almost destroyed itself knocking out the Japanese in thirty-five different battles in Burma in World War II—five of them major. "We weren't even a shadow of that legendary force," added Travis, "but I liked the comparison. Frank Merrill's immortals were awarded, to a man, the Bronze Star for unusual valor."

You have to love that Green Berets–SEALs rivalry, Army vs. Navy, and they'd all lay down their lives for each other, any time. But by anyone's standards, the Green Berets and the Rangers made a fabulous effort that first day. They climbed five thousand feet up and over the peak of the mountain before leveling out and heading downward.

But on the following night, at 2100, the thunderstorm broke, and the guys were out there on the mountain, trying to hunker down behind rocks, anywhere to find shelter from the driving rain.

When the downpour eased slightly, they set off again, pushing on toward the far-distant uplands around Sabray, where they believed they would find the missing SEALs. Midnight found them on slightly flatter ground, still going, sliding, squelching, fighting for footholds, checking the waypoints as the pounding rain rose and fell in intensity.

Gulab's own little army made its slow, painful progress up through the woods until finally it came to a small flight of rough-hewn steps cut into the rock. He'd been this way before, but not very often. It was a wild area where even the herds of tribal goats do not pass. Gulab looked at those steps and thought to himself, *This will not be my favorite part of the journey, trying to push Marcus up there.*

But there was no choice. No one wanted to go back. They had to keep pushing forward. And the two porters got behind him and let the American fall back slightly so that he was effectively sitting on their shoulders. Then they pushed, edging him upward.

On the fourth step, however, Gulab received one of the biggest surprises of his life. An armed Afghani fighter, his AK-47 leveled straight at him, was staring him in the face. The man was dressed in combat gear, looked as if he'd had a very rough time, and was poised to open fire.

This, Gulab felt, was one hell of a way to die: too late to grab his rifle because he was hanging onto the back of an infidel. Then, in just a fraction of a second, Gulab saw foreign words on the guy's headgear, and the one he recognized was *Bush*—the name of the American president.

In a moment of blind panic, he grasped for a word to stop anyone from opening fire, especially at Marcus, who was dressed in Afghan clothes and looked like a full-blown Taliban terrorist.

Gulab dismissed the idea of shouting "Marcus!" because he did not even know if that was his real name. But he was staring at the warrior's headgear badge, and it was screaming loudly that this guy was either an American or fighting with the Americans.

Gulab's mind went blank, and the only thing he could think of was that huge tattoo on Marcus's back. And somehow he remembered those blue numbers engraved into the SEAL's upper arm: 2-2-8.

He thrust his empty hand into the air and yelled at the top of his lungs, "*Two-two-eight! It's two-two-eight!*" Gulab had not the slightest idea what this signified. But it rang some distant bell with someone. The soldier with the helmet stopped dead in his tracks and lowered his rifle.

"American? American?" he called out. And then two more really rough-looking characters came bursting through the trees, guns raised. Gulab just kept bellowing, "*Two-two-eight! It's two-two-eight!*"

The new man was big, black, and obviously American. For Gulab, the world stood still, and so did his heart, just with pure relief that no one opened fire. The American looked at Marcus and then his face split into an enormous smile.

"Marcus?" he said. He whipped around and roared, "It's Marcus, guys! We got him! We got him! Right here we got him!"

Gulab never understood the English language with such fluency as he did at that moment. "And," he says, "I have to say, I never have since!"

Anyone could see what this meant to them. The smiling soldier ran forward and took Marcus into his arms, and as he stepped into the clearing, tears streamed down Marcus's face. Tears of laughter? Tears of joy? Tears of pure relief? Who knows? But it was a life-changing moment for the American.

And rapidly, US troops came swarming out from the under-growth—big, tough, heavily armed men, much bigger than Gulab's own people. They were all laughing and moving forward to shake Marcus's hand. He was absolutely unable to speak, and the black man who'd grabbed him first just kept saying over and over, "It's okay, buddy. It's okay now. We got you. You're good."

This was an unimaginable scene for Gulab: all of them with sev-eral days' stubble on their faces, covered in mud, completely dishev-eled and beat up. It was obvious that the men had been out for days crossing the mountain, since before the big thunderstorm. Gulab was frankly amazed they had not been attacked by Shah's troops as soon as they came within striking distance.

Someone explained that they were trying to get a message through to Texas: "Gotta tell your mom you're okay!" It was pandemonium in that clearing. The incredible focus of the overnight mission, bro-ken by the joyful reunion. But at first, not everyone was friendly. The Americans thought that Marcus had been kidnapped. But Gulab watched Marcus explaining what he'd done for him, and soon they understood that not only was he a friendly, he was a critical asset.

After their quick burst of excitement upon finding Marcus, the Americans returned to their calm efficiency. The US medic ordered a stretcher party to move in and carry Marcus out of the forest and up to higher ground, where everyone could see.

And there a US professional went to work. Gulab remembers him well. His name was Travis, and he cut away Marcus's bandages, cleaned the wounds, applied new antiseptic cream, and produced spotless new dressings, which he applied expertly. Then he made Marcus take the first of a course of antibiotics. At Marcus's insistence, they allowed Gulab to stay with him.

The Afghani was filled with admiration. These men had been out there for five days, in shocking conditions, and yet somehow, in hundreds of square miles of rough, wild, mountainous country, they'd found him—walked right up to the very patch of ground where Gulab had led him.

That could have been a fluke. But it really wasn't. The US Special Forces had a mission to find Marcus, and they accomplished it, guessing correctly that if the enemy were on the mountain across from the village, Marcus would somehow be in a different part. They were following a track down while Gulab pushed his way forward. The moment of collision was an example of truly expert soldiering and navigation. The mujahideen commanders would have congratulated the men of the United States.

While Marcus's wounds were being attended to, the Americans made a makeshift headquarters up there by the high goat pens. Marcus was trying to inform them that they were virtually surrounded by a Taliban dragnet. Gulab had told them to expect Ahmad Shah's maximum attack force to number maybe three hundred.

There were more than a hundred US Special Forces, including the doctor, and the three-to-one odds did not seem to worry anyone in the slightest. They were very confident, probably based on reports of the terrible damage inflicted on Shah's troops by Marcus's small team of four. And Shah, having already experienced just how lethal and destructive American airpower could be, would never want another direct confrontation with US firepower.

Eventually, after about an hour, the US forces decided to go down to the village and set up some type of headquarters. Gulab led them down the hillside and helped them settle into a few houses that might not have been the most comfortable situation they'd ever been in, but they were secure, and a guard was placed on duty at various points on the edge of Sabray, facing the mountains.

There, behind those thick mud walls, the Americans worked on, listening to Marcus, drawing diagrams and maps, marking out where the Taliban were encamped. Gulab could see their planning was meticulous. And he spent a half hour talking to Marcus, who was very tired but still tried to explain to his weeklong host just who these fierce and efficient fighters from America actually were.

By now, Marcus was aware of Gulab's military background and his obvious field rank. And the Afghani was making endless attempts to find out about these scruffy-looking rescuers. It was obvious these men truly interested him. But how to explain the heritage of these historic US Special Forces to a man who barely understood one word of English? "Green Beret," for instance, had him totally confused. Gulab started off from the premise that it was an unripe blackberry, because Marcus had told him the English word for the fruit he was eating when Ahmad Shah showed up. And "Rangers" was probably worse. He thought it was a variation on the word *stranger* or *danger*, which he thought he understood.

Gulab and Marcus sat together and tried to communicate while the guys made their evacuation plans, and finally Gulab was convinced that the Green Berets had nothing to do with blackberries. All through the afternoon, they watched the US personnel opening up the communications, pinpointing the Taliban army, and plainly making plans for a dangerous exit from Sabray for both men and their rescuers.

Marcus made it clear that Gulab was coming with him, because he could not possibly be left behind alone to face the Taliban's hit men. They had sworn to kill him and his family, and Marcus was in no mood to test whether or not they meant it.

He actually believed that Shah would have sent in many men just to make sure that the man who saved the infidel murderer died at the hands of an Islamic force. It would be a pure revenge killing for the dozens of turbaned warriors he and the other Redwings had wiped out on the mountain the previous week.

Gulab was leaving simply because no one, with a clear conscience, could possibly have consigned him to his certain fate. Marcus made quite certain everyone understood that.

Gulab noticed during this awkward exchange that one word kept coming up over and over: *opium*. Marcus said it several times, and the US commanders said it frequently. In turn, they passed it on to the young officer who was manning the communications, and he, in turn, passed it on to whomever was on the other end of the line.

At first, Gulab thought they might be forming some kind of a drug cartel, and he wondered about informing them that they had just missed the harvest. However, Marcus took great trouble in explaining to him that they were discussing the Sabray opium field below the village, the only place sufficiently flat to possibly land a military helicopter and then take off again.

However, even someone as unskilled in air warfare as Gulab could understand this was a dreadful idea. For a start, there was a granite mountain wall on one side of the field, and on the other, a sheer drop of probably two thousand feet to the valley floor. In front stood a couple of sizable trees. But there was nowhere else.

The Americans would need a superhuman pilot to get them out. The slightest error coming in to land on that narrow field could be fatal to everyone. Plus, no one was absolutely thrilled about a big US military helicopter blowing itself up, against the wall, right on the perimeter of the village.

Gulab had reached the point where he had no idea about his future, if he had any. Marcus had made it clear he was leaving with him, since he could not possibly stay in Sabray. But he did not want to go all the way to America, leaving behind his wife and family. He assumed that he would go to a US base and perhaps be given work there. And he knew his days guarding Marcus were drawing to a close. Soon the American would leave, and Gulab had no idea when he would see him again, if ever.

Even with a vast succession of hand signals and demonstrations, Marcus had communicated very little about himself, except about where he came from: this hot, flat American state of Texas, where there was only one star in the sky and where a half-crazed American Communist had gunned down President John F. Kennedy from a sixth-floor window in the Texas School Book Depository. He also understood that Marcus's parents had worked with horses, and they lived on a small ranch.

Marcus had explained his brother, Morgan, was somehow the same as him and was also a member of the US Special Forces. Both Luttrells had been in military training since they were very young. But they were running and swimming and climbing while Gulab was gunning down Russians with his dushka-mounted machine gun.

They'd both dodged a lot of bullets in their time, but how Marcus was not shot on the mountain during the battle remained a deep mystery. Gulab had heard from several sources that all three of the other SEALs had been shot many, many times, but not Marcus. No one hit him except for a sniper when he was trying to get away.

Gulab wished at the time of the rescue that he knew him better—knew more about him personally. They really liked each other, even though they did not, after all, have an awful lot to go on besides their warrior bond.

But now they stood together. And, their gods willing, they'd somehow soon be airlifted out—the American never to return. Gulab understood that he might not come back, either, and would have to move his entire family into whatever new residence he could establish.

And that might be difficult, since his family and all of their ancestors had lived in Sabray for more than two thousand years—before even the Christian prophet, Jesus Christ, was born.

The afternoon wore on, and Gulab was more and more impressed with Captain Travis, the medical chief. He later learned that Ranger medics are nothing short of walking hospitals and probably the most respected medics in the US military.

No platoon goes anywhere without one. Men like Travis are trained to treat battlefield injuries. They can swiftly establish a field clinic. They can prescribe medicine, vaccinate, and perform minor surgery. They can identify bacteria in contaminated water wells, and even deliver babies. Gulab watched him make Marcus feel better and better.

Communications from this new Rangers–Navy SEAL HQ in Sabray never stopped. Gulab could not understand anything they said, and it was impossible to help them much, except with drawings of the entrenched Taliban positions on the mountain.

All around the village, the American guards were in position, especially on the Taliban side. Like Marcus, they attracted the kids, who were always running up to them, and shouting "Hello, Dr. Marcus!" which they assumed was an all-purpose US greeting.

The Americans were really nice to them, and it was hard for Gulab to accept that here were these big, genial people from across the world, guarding his village from a section of armed, thuggish Pashtuns, whom almost no one liked.

No one ordered the children to return home, because their presence, standing and laughing alongside these US soldiers, was a major plus. The Taliban might be stupid enough to attack the American Rangers, but they surely understood that one stray bullet hitting one of the children would set everyone within a ten-mile radius against them forever.

All afternoon, Shah's army did not attack. But as the soft light of dusk set in, things began to change dramatically. A succession of US fighter-bombers flew over the region, screaming across the skies directly above at high speed and, at first, high altitude. The whole place shook when they split the sound barrier.

It shook a great deal more in the ensuing couple of hours when the US air attack increased, and they began to batter the slopes opposite the village with bombs, rockets, and gunfire. It was as if the military had finally had enough of Ahmad Shah and decided to quiet him once and for all.

It was the kind of onslaught you associate with a World War II urban destruction program over Germany or London. An outsider stumbling across this bombardment might think there would be no survivors. And the accuracy of the bombardment was outstanding. They hit the Taliban slopes and nothing else. No bombs or rockets hit the village.

Families hastened to get inside undercover. And everyone realized that this was it. This was what that afternoon of endless communications had been for. The Rangers and the Green Berets had orchestrated this attack. Gulab had watched them sending messages, signals on their computers, probably GPS readings. These were plainly precision attacks, and the Taliban must have sustained heavy casualties again.

Of course, any experienced combat commander understands that bombing a wild mountainous area does not inflict quite the 100 percent death toll you might think. Fighting men find places to take cover: behind rocks and trees, in gullies, away from the straight, low lines of the actual blast.

Marcus was a prime example of that, somehow avoiding the Taliban onslaught of grenades while the Americans were pinned down and taking casualties. They slammed him in the leg. But they never killed him.

As the explosions shook the mountain, Gulab returned to his constant thought about the Taliban and their Al Qaeda friends. As a group, they had caused all this; they alone had caused the world to go to war.

When those hijacked aircrafts crashed into the World Trade Center, it very swiftly became clear that a president like George Bush was not going to just sit there and accept it. When he unleashed his gigantic military on Afghanistan, all the Taliban had to do was betray this crazed Saudi, bin Laden, and tell the Americans where he was hiding. They could have offered guidance and assistance to the world's most powerful nation, which had been such a friend to Afghanistan.

But they made the wrong decision. They would not betray bin Laden, this dangerous, reckless foreigner, cowering in the mountains with his ridiculous "army." The Taliban caused havoc by their actions, and when they first asked Gulab to betray Marcus, he told Shah to his face, "You would not hand over bin Laden. And I will not hand over Marcus."

Everyone sat quietly in the village through that evening, but the Rangers were endlessly in communication with their base during the US attack on the mountain, perhaps speaking to the pilots. But at ten o'clock that night, they ordered everyone down to the opium field.

The Rangers asked Gulab to lead the way, and they all walked the hundred yards down the steep hill and onto the flat, very dusty ground, dried out now after the harvest and the rainstorm. He and his nephew, Norzamund, who had been helping to guard Marcus from the start, assisted the Americans in carrying him over the roughest parts.

When they finally arrived, they headed for the far wall and sat down with their backs against it. There were intermittent explosions, but the Taliban guns were silent, for the moment. It did occur to Marcus they might all be dead.

The shapes of the high pinnacles stood black against the mountains under the dark sky. Gulab was sorrowful, wondering if he would ever pass this way again. It seemed incomprehensible that this place, beloved of his ancestors for centuries, would be lost to him—that he would not see it again.

The personal threats against him were real. And the threats against his vulnerable family were worse. But Gulab had to go, and, subsequently, so did they. He sat thinking about everything he had always loved up there: the pure blue, cloudless skies in summer; the sight of the faraway peaks capped with snow; the solitude; the sense of belonging; the certainty of Pashtun survival.

For him, there could never be anywhere else. And should this all be taken away, it would be as if a light from the center of the earth had somehow gone out. He was forever a mountain man in a landlocked country. The oceans and fertile lowlands would always be strange to him. He might admire them. He might even like them. But he could never be *of them,* as he was of the high peaks of the Hindu Kush.

This harsh, rugged end of the Himalayas has always embraced everyone who lived there, protecting them from invasion and conquest. Since the beginning of time, these mighty walls, some more than twenty-three thousand feet high, have encircled the villages, guarded the families, and isolated the communities from a world they did not really understand. No one ever dominated the men of the Hindu Kush; no one ever won a lasting war up there. Not against the Pashtun tribes.

But now, thanks to the Taliban, all might be lost for such people. As Gulab sat there with Marcus, he thought that his own back was against the wall more significantly than for any other of the brave warriors who sat alongside him. He alone faced the loss of everything he had ever known.

He sat there in a kind of daze, staring ahead at the mountain, watching the tracers from the passing US gunships, cursing the very ground upon which the Taliban walked.

Instructions from the Rangers had been precise. It was obvious that the helicopter would arrive soon. And, for all of the above reasons, Gulab viewed that prospect with mixed feelings. To be taken away from here was nearly impossible for him to imagine. But to remain here without permanent US protection was out of the question.

He badly wanted to talk to Marcus about how he felt, and to discuss with him what future there was for him and his family. But the endless problem was still there, of course. Great friends though they now were, they could not speak to each other. Especially on subjects as complex as this.

7

"NEGATIVE BURN!...NEGATIVE BURN!"

Neither Gulab nor Marcus had the remotest idea of what was going on, except that they were sitting in the middle of a US bombardment of the mountain, like a couple of guys waiting for a bus. They were, however, both holding machine guns, ready to lash out at anything that threatened them.

In fact, there was an enormous amount going on back at the base in preparation for one of the biggest and most dangerous mountain air rescues ever undertaken by the US military.

This was a specialist operation. The 920th Rescue Squad shares its headquarters with the Forty-Fifth Space Wing at Patrick Air Force Base on the Banana River, on the east coast of central Florida. Its two-mile-long main runway stands twelve miles south of Cape Canaveral. The 920th has participated in many space adventures, frequently hooking returning astronauts and their space capsules out of the ocean.

It is actually an official part of Air Force Space Command, and in recent years, the very name 920th has become a byword for hair-raising air–sea rescue heroism. During Hurricane Katrina in 2005, the 920th was credited with saving more than a thousand lives, flying low over windblown, dangerous waters, sending their men down the heavy lines from the helicopters, and hauling people to safety.

The iron men who exit the helos and swing down to the rescue are known as the pararescuemen, or the PJs (that's pararescue jumpers). No one in all of US military history has been anything less than thrilled by their sudden arrival on the scene. Their creed sends shivers down the spine: "It is my duty to save lives and to aid the injured . . . These things I do, that others may live."

Airman Second Class Duane D. Hackney, the most decorated airman in the entire history of the US Air Force, was a pararescueman. He received the Air Force Cross for his actions while recovering a downed pilot under heavy fire in the jungles of North Vietnam in 1967.

Hackney carried him up and into the aircraft, and when the helicopter was hit, he gave the wounded man his own parachute, saying afterward, "That's my job. Rescuing people." He was the first enlisted man—and, at twenty, the youngest—to receive that award, and he earned twenty-seven others for valor, for a total of more than seventy decorations in all.

There were other heroes like Duane in the 920th, and these were the guys Gulab and Marcus awaited. No one else could do what they could do. No one else had the background to put down in the Sabray opium field with about two feet of clearance on either side.

The 920th was stationed in Bagram, and a lot of Special Forces had many reasons to be thankful for them. Everyone just liked knowing those guys were there if push came to shove. And in Marcus's case, it surely had. He still couldn't walk.

He wouldn't know for months exactly how far the ripples from Operation Redwings had extended. At this point, he had a rough idea that the Chinook had gone down with everyone on board—Gulab had tried to tell him. But the first source was the Taliban rabble, who had all shouted and laughed, sliding one open hand over their own throats and making circular helicopter blade motions with the other.

The SEAL commanders swiftly understood that the 920th were the exact right men. If anyone could find the downed Chinook and then possibly Marcus, it was that Air Force Rescue Wing.

They were commanded by the tall, craggy Lieutenant Colonel Jeffrey L. Macrander, a veteran command pilot with more than 4,600 hours' flying experience in five different aircraft. He was a military scientist and a weapons expert destined for personal high command. For some outlandish reason, he was known universally as Skinny.

Commander of the second rescue helicopter was Major Jeffrey Val Peterson, a highly educated airman who had attended both Brigham Young and Arizona State Universities and earned an MBA in business administration. He and his crew had participated in over a hundred combat missions in Afghanistan, pulling wounded people off mountains, out of deep valleys, and clear of firefights.

For some reason, he acquired the nickname of Spanky, but Peterson also had a huge reputation as a Special Ops pilot, commanding one of the most advanced and sophisticated helicopters ever built: the Sikorsky HH-60 Pave Hawk, with its twin turbo-shaft engines, a toned-up derivative of the legendary UH-60 Black Hawk.

Like Skinny and Spanky, this baby is a true specialist. It's built for combat search and rescue, or, as the Air Force prefers, "recovery of personnel under stressful conditions, day or night, in hostile environments." Marcus's predicament slotted right into that job description.

Although a cousin of the Black Hawk, the Pave Hawk is a highly modified version, featuring an upgraded communications and navigation suite, with an integrated navigation/global positioning system, satellite comms, and secure voice. It's like a flying NASA ops room—which I guess it really is. PAVE stands for precision avionics vectoring equipment.

You almost need a scientific degree just to fly the thing, with its automatic flight controls, special lighting for night vision goggles (NVGs), forward-looking infrared system for low-level ops at night, and a personnel locating system. It's got weather radar in color, anti-icing on the rotors, machine guns, and an antimissile system, dispensing a chaff countermeasure. It also has a hoist capable of lifting six hundred pounds from a hover height of two hundred feet. The Pave Hawks are the sixty-five-foot-long workhorses of USAF Rescue. It is an awesome helicopter, with a main rotor diameter of almost fifty-four feet, and the ability to fly nonstop for fourteen hours in any weather, night or day, cruising at 184 miles per hour for, if necessary, 375 miles.

The SH-60 carries a six-man crew: two pilots, a flight engineer, a gunner, and two pararescuemen (PJs) in the back—this would be a couple of guys who passed one of the most brutal indoctrinations in the US military: the Air Force "Superman School" in San Antonio, Texas. It's modeled on SEAL training and is reputed to be just as tough. Maybe, nearly. But no one is as tough as the SEALs.

Almost all search and rescue ops are conducted under the cover of darkness; by hugging the ground at night, it's nearly impossible for the enemy to see or hear them approaching. In the Pave Hawk, they can see in the dark. Their state-of-the-art night vision goggles amplify the available light from the moon and the stars about five thousand times. There have never been NVGs as good as that, and everything appears phosphorus green. That's by design, for the human eye can identify more shades of green than any other color.

Skinny and Spanky had already been up on the mountainside looking for Marcus and his fellow SEALs. They took off from Bagram at 1840 just before nightfall on Wednesday evening, June 29, while Marcus was nearly bleeding to death on the mountain.

Exactly where Marcus was and where the 920th guys were during this time is a bit of a mystery. But Marcus, in those earlier hours of the night, was making very slow progress up the mountain, while they must have been searching the valley where the wreckage of the Chinook was scattered on the hillside.

They definitely found it, but it was in very small pieces, and they located it through the heat-seeking infrared system, flying close to the mountain wall, back and forth, back and forth, searching for any sign of life. But, of course, there was none. No one could have possibly gotten out of that crash alive.

Skinny piloted the first helicopter, and Spanky flew the second. They always work in twos, and when they fix on a target for rescue, one goes in hard and low, and then banks away steeply in an attempt to draw enemy fire. That's when the second Pave Hawk goes in real low and makes the landing. In this case, Spanky would be the one making the rescue.

But after hours of searching, they had not located the missing Redwings, or, rather, Redwing. But they had picked up on the emergency frequency a faint clicking, which must have been Marcus's beacon. Anyone could understand how jumpy they must have been—had the Taliban grabbed that beacon off one of the dead SEALs and were now using it to coax yet another US helo into rocket range?

Skinny was quoted as saying, "We were just hoping that beacon was still with one of the SEALs. The Taliban had already shown if you fly close enough, they are capable of shooting you down. And this was not a distant possibility. We were searching the exact same area where they'd just done it."

No one wanted to abandon the search. Spanky recalls those hours: "It was coming up to midnight, and we were still getting that faint clicking on the frequency. I just hated the idea of leaving someone alone down there, but nothing was coming up on the infrared.

"I remember flying through that dark, right up against the mountain wall, peering through my NVGs, my copilot glued to the IR. I kept saying to myself, or anyone else who might be listening, 'If there's someone there, please, please make yourself known, anything you can do, just let us know. We are United States Air Force rescue. We'll do anything just to get one of the PJs down there, pick you up, and get you out.'"

Spanky's copilot, Lieutenant Dave "Gonzo" Gonzales, kept thinking over and over, "They gotta be close by; they gotta be close by." But they all knew it was like searching for a needle in a haystack, seven or eight thousand feet high in the mountains.

Their iron determination applied especially to a truly fearless pararescue man, Staff Sergeant Chris "Checky" Piercecchi. A highly trained trauma specialist, he'd be first out of the helicopter, if and when they located Marcus, and dropped down into the landing zone. If they had to hover, Checky would be the man coming down the rope.

But the clouds never lifted. It remained pitch-dark all night, and this added to the danger for the rescuemen. The NVGs had no heavenly lights to amplify their instruments, since they were flying way below the clouds and relying entirely on the heat-seeking camera to negotiate the mountain passes.

The camera can detect heat even when there is absolutely no light. Which is a miracle, since up there, when the ground has been baked all day by the sun, the rock registers as a glaring image in the cockpit, and nothing is easy to spot.

But neither their equipment nor their determination could find Marcus as he crawled up the escarpment below them. They kept going until it was almost time for the sun to push up above the peaks.

And they dared not risk a daytime sighting by the Afghani missile men. As dawn cracked the dark skies apart in the Hindu Kush, the two rescue helicopters reluctantly turned back to the west and headed home to Bagram, without the lost SEAL.

Every member of that rescue crew remembers the somber mood in the helos. The 920th is not used to failure, and in this case, the men felt they'd been very near to finding the missing Redwing but never quite nailed it.

It did, of course, have a lot to do with Murphy's Law. They were searching around the SEALs' last known position—standard practice in any military or naval operation. There was only the crash and Mikey's phone call to guide them.

Since those two events, Marcus had been hurrying away from the area, covering a distance that surprised even him. By the time Gulab found him, he was about seven miles from that original mountain location, so the rescuers were starting their search in the wrong place. No fault of theirs. Even the tribal goat-herders were amazed at how far the giant Texan had gone.

Everyone was beginning to assume that Marcus was dead. And a couple more days went by, during which time he had passed into the care of Gulab.

The men from the 920th had previously been looking forward to this Fourth of July weekend. Spanky had been scheduled to go home to the States, to his very pretty wife and four boys. That was called off the moment he was chosen by Skinny to fly one of the Pave Hawks up into the mountains.

Although many people thought there were no Redwing survivors, Spanky was not one of them. He had heard in the cockpit that faint clicking of Luttrell's beam. That sound kept him awake at night.

He also felt that he, Skinny, and the boys had been close to finding the SEAL; that they'd been forced to give up because daybreak was approaching, as well as low fuel and inaccurate GPS numbers.

The mission of the 920th was never to capture a place, or storm anything, or win firefights. It was always to rescue people. Nothing more. And the events of the night of June 29–30 had left a bad taste in everyone's mouth. It was not their fault. It was just the way the cards fell.

But Major Spanky was quietly longing for another shot, just to get the Pave Hawk fired up and head right back up there to locate the missing SEAL. He waited at Bagram with all the other rescue crewmen, hoping for a word, a signal—any sign there was still a mission to complete up in those mountains.

Colonel Skinny was of the same mind. He also knew all too well about the clicking beacon. As the overall commander, he needed to assess the danger level of flying back into hostile Taliban country when it was so difficult to see anything below, and their NVGs might not work again because of the cloud cover.

The objective of the mission would not change. It was still to pick up Marcus, if he were still alive, and then find the bodies of the other three.

"It was," said the colonel, "a huge responsibility. Our job was to get these men back to their families, dead or alive. Even before we left for the second leg of the operation, I was praying—a simple prayer, but the best I could do: 'Oh, Lord, please, please do not let me screw this up.'"

All through that Friday, July 1, the guys waited. The Pave Hawks were fueled up, every operational part checked, the electronics tested. No two military helicopters were ever in better shape for an operation that had yet to be given the green light.

The SEAL ops room was receiving no word from the Taliban battle zone apart from brief reports on US Air Force activities in the area, and the Rangers were not yet within striking distance of the village. Pilots sometimes thought there was a faint electronic clicking from Sabray, but nothing definite.

There was certainly nothing to countermand Colonel Skinny's orders from High Command, which meant broadly: "The United States cannot afford to lose another helicopter on that damned mountain."

Like all their other meals, dinner for the 920th was a gloomy occasion. No one had heard anything since they'd returned at dawn on Thursday morning. No one wanted the rescue mission called off. But there was plainly no point in charging back up there with no more information and guidance than they'd had the first time.

And now it was Saturday night. Back home in the United States, the Fourth of July weekend was under way. Men who should have been with their families just sat around reading, watching television, not speaking much. Just thinking, worrying, their minds locked on those steep, cold hillsides up there in the Hindu Kush.

Each of them understood that several dozen Taliban killers, armed with antiaircraft missiles, were hunkered down in their mountain bunkers, waiting just for them. But the part that counted much more for the 920th rescuers was the upsetting possibility that somewhere up there was a freezing-cold American hero, all alone, trying to stay alive, and probably praying to the same God as Colonel Skinny.

If they were cleared to take off, it might be lethal. It could be the last mission any of them would ever attempt. But their primary thoughts were always of the rescue, not the risks. And the words of the PJ creed echoed silently among them—the words they were sworn to uphold: "that others may live."

Midnight came and went. The rescuers were waiting one hour at a time. And the time crawled by. Sometimes they dozed off, but they were all on a self-imposed standby, waiting for something to happen—anything—just to let them know there was a target up there in the mountains. Someone in need of help.

Shortly after 0430, with the pale light of dawn breaking over the mountain peaks, they got it. A message came in from the small US base at Asadabad. An elderly tribesman had arrived at the gates, and he had brought a handwritten message, written and signed by one of the four original Redwings: Marcus Luttrell.

Maluk, Gulab's seventy-five-year-old brother-in-law, had made the twenty-mile trek over the mountains, with the news the entire US military had been waiting for. Marcus was alive, and the letter he had written told them what they needed to know.

He was in the care of the villagers of Sabray—he had written in the GPS numbers—and confirmed what they probably knew: the place was being blockaded by the Taliban army, which was intent on killing him and anyone who might object.

Marcus did tell them that he was pretty badly wounded in more places than he could count, but he was definitely breathing. The one thing no one knew was precisely when the village elder had arrived at Asadabad. The US Army had obviously spent some time checking out poor old Maluk, who'd done a lot for Marcus—such as saving his life, twice—and did not deserve rough treatment.

But the US guards needed to be sure. Maluk might even have been a Taliban suicide bomber with an improvised explosive device, or IED. Anyhow, they believed him in the end, assumed the letter was genuine, and alerted those who needed to know: the battered, soaking Rangers on the hill. And the rescue guys at the Bagram base.

And very swiftly, the operation to save Marcus Luttrell swept into place. Within hours, they had satellite photos of Sabray on the network. By late morning, the helicopter commanders were finalizing their strategy.

And a squad of towering heroes, with names like something out of an old Western movie, were gearing up for action: Skinny, Spanky, Gonzo, and Checky. Four men whose bravery Marcus will never forget.

On Saturday morning, July 2, the sun rose out of the eastern Himalayas and cast its mountain light on Alexander the Great's ancient city of Bagram.

Hard alongside this storied place, the giant US military air base, home to thousands of American troops, braced itself for another burning hot day—even here, five thousand feet above sea level in the foothills of the five-hundred-mile long Afghani range.

Right now, before 0530, the air was cool, but all along the lines and lines of barracks huts (B-huts), half-awake military personnel understood one thing that would set this day apart: they were going in tonight, the rescue guys, to try to grab the big, lost Texan SEAL Marcus Luttrell from under the hooked nose of the Taliban chief, Ahmad Shah.

Everyone in Bagram knew about this unfolding tragedy in the mountains. Everyone knew about the past week's battle, and the helicopter crash, which had added up to the worst day in US Special Forces history. And everyone knew the Rangers were still just short of the local area.

The 920th Wing's rescue helos were going in alone—into the teeth of Taliban gunfire and rockets, and into some of the most dangerous flying country in the world: the massive steep-sided rock gorges of the Hindu Kush.

It might have been just another rescue mission for the Americans, but this one was different. Ahmad Shah had dealt the SEALs a savage blow: not a general attack on the West through the murderous destruction of the World Trade Center four years previously. This one hit even closer to home: a deliberate attack on America's most beloved fighting force. And eleven of them were dead, plus eight other US Special Forces.

And right now, there seemed to be just one survivor from that infamous day. And that survivor might also be dead. No one knew. But everyone cared. And when Skinny and Spanky lifted off from the main Bagram runway tonight, they would not be alone, because, in so many ways, every last man on that base would go with them. No rescue operation ever carried a greater burden of hopes and good wishes. To Skinny and Spanky, it seemed that the outcome of the entire Afghan war hung in the balance as they clattered up through the passes, sweeping the valley for a sign of the missing Marcus.

And right now, even as the Afghan sun burned through cool, clear skies, the ops room over at the Special Forces section was alive with information. The satellite maps were up on the big screen, there was now an open line to the Rangers, still hacking their way across the mountain to the west of Sabray.

And still the pilots were calling in traces of that faint clicking being transmitted weakly by Marcus's beacon—jammed in the window frame and still valiantly sending up its unanswered electronic plea for help.

It was marvelous to have the photographs from space, illuminating at last the place where the lost SEAL was sheltering. But the images were not all encouraging. For a start, there was nowhere, anywhere, around the village, high or low, east or west, that any pilot, in his wildest dreams, could possibly land a helicopter without crashing and rolling down the mountain.

There was hardly an inch of flat ground. The guys in the ops room were gazing at a rock and boulder–strewn moonscape with high trees and a cluster of maybe a hundred square, mud-brick houses, built tightly together around a narrow street not wide enough to park a couple of motor bikes, never mind a sixty-five-foot-long Pave Hawk helicopter with a fifty-four-foot rotor span.

Computers were taking the images and making them three-dimensional, converting the helicopter into a line-drawn diagram, demonstrating the tight distances and dangers in this awful country. It was like an architect's plan come to life—accurate, orange-lit, worked by military information-technology wizards, all trying to plot a way to fly the helicopter into the outer edges of the village.

They tried every which way, all through the morning, and in the end arrived at precisely the same conclusion that Gulab had reached the previous day: it's the opium field or nothing. And Spanky was gazing with a certain amount of horror at the map and the potential landing zone: not total horror, because nothing looks as bad from an ops office as it will from the cockpit of a piercingly loud helicopter, swerving in a mountain wind, in the pitch-dark, with a two-hundred-foot-high granite wall three feet to the left.

Nonetheless, it was still horror. And it was tight—as tight a landing as either rescue pilot had ever seen, with a rock wall on one side, a two-thousand-foot sheer drop to the valley floor on the other, and a small grove of trees to the rear. The hazards to the left and right represented instant death. The trees? Don't even think about what might happen if the slashing rotor blades hit one of those.

In some ways, this was the mission these teams had been preparing for ever since they joined the Rescue Wing. But if it should go wrong, it would cast an everlasting shadow on their whole lives.

Still, an everlasting shadow was a whole lot better than getting incinerated in a burning helo. Tumultuous thoughts clambered through all of their minds; some positive, some negative, all confused—the opportunity, the danger, the glory, and the terror of a screwup.

This was the moment every combat rescue pilot dreams of and yet dreads. This is the day when each one of them puts years of training to the test.

"In the end," said Spanky, "none of it mattered. The objective remained pure and simple: to fly Marcus Luttrell out of there, hopefully alive. And every one of us knew that.

"That day, we listened to a thousand assessments of the problems, and I paid deep attention to every one of them. But we were still going. I knew that, and so did everyone else. When night fell, we would lift off and head right back up to those mountains. If Marcus was alive, we were not coming back without him."

Focal point of their studies, all day long, was that landing zone in the opium field. And by midafternoon, another major breakthrough occurred when the Rangers made contact. They'd not only arrived on the hillside opposite the village but also had moved in and were sending in the GPS numbers. In their estimation, the landing was difficult but not impossible.

Marcus was alive. He was badly hurt, but he wasn't in danger of dying, and they had a top Green Beret corpsman tending his wounds.

There were some good guys in Sabray, especially Marcus's Afghani bodyguard, who had high authority among the villagers.

The Rangers would have Marcus and his man down there at the LZ, or landing zone, by 2200. They wanted a barrage of high explosives blasted onto the western slope, where the heavy guns of the Taliban faced the opium field. And they wanted it a full half hour before the ETA (estimated time of arrival). They were concerned but not worried. Typical Green Berets.

"Anytime the boss wants us to knock the shit out of these Taliban jerks, just let us know. Meanwhile, keep 'em well occupied from the air while the rescue guys do their thing. Marcus says 'Hi,' and could someone reserve him a cheeseburger?"

Long before they released details of the US air armada that would accompany the rescue helicopters, they established and confirmed that the mission would proceed under standard tactics. The two Pave Hawks would fly together, commanded by Colonel Macrander and Major Peterson.

They would operate in close quarters, protecting and covering for each other, as they had practiced a thousand times in the Arizona desert. With a known enemy lying in wait, they would make the journey in the fastest possible time, at speeds reaching two hundred miles per hour.

When they reached the zone, they would go in swiftly, with the lead helo making a fast pass over the LZ, trying to draw enemy fire, and then pulling out hard and high. This would hopefully leave the airspace clear for the second Pave Hawk to swoop in for the pickup.

Major Spanky had heard all this so many times. That was the way the Rescue Wing operated. But he suspected that Skinny would elect to make the pickup himself. That, however, was not going to happen. Mindful of the difficult cloud cover and the lack of light up there when they were searching for the Chinook, the senior commander elected to go in first himself. Then he would hurl a glow stick right into the middle of the landing zone, to illuminate Spanky's way.

At that precise moment, the mild-natured, amiable major from Arizona understood for the first time that he, Spanky, had been selected to pilot the helicopter that would pick up Marcus Luttrell. He stared once more at the big screen and the virtual image of the Pave Hawk trying to make it down onto a "shelf" carved into the mountain.

The shelf looked about as big as a chessboard. So far as the Rescue Wing commander could tell, this would have tested the edge of the envelope in the southwestern US desert in daylight. But in the Hindu Kush at night, with a bunch of wild men trying to get a missile shot into you, well . . .

"That's when my heart sank," he said later. "That was when I shot right out of my comfort level. I was concentrating on that brief as if my life depended on it, and within a few seconds, I realized it might do just that. And I glared at that screen, studying everything I could commit to memory about that landing zone.

"But, curiously, it was not the terrain on the mountain that jumped to the front of my mind. It was the angle of approach—the landing angle—where there is so much margin for even the slightest error . . .

"The task of the first helo going in required pinpoint precision to drop that glow stick in exactly the right place at high speed. And Skinny was a master. The function of the second pilot, me, to land a ten-ton hunk of howling, vibrating machinery onto uneven ground as gently as a falling lotus blossom, that was altogether different. At least it was in my mind. As I mentioned before, right here my concentration was total."

Honored to have been chosen, utterly aware of the dangers, Major Peterson, like so many warriors before him, suddenly had thoughts of home, thoughts of Penny, his wife, and his four little boys. Not for the first time that day, he offered a prayer to anyone who might be paying attention: "Please don't let me screw this up."

Meanwhile, the US Air Force was preparing once more for a huge combat rescue operation, which had inevitably shouldered its way to the forefront of everyone's mind. It was hard for anyone to know the scariest part, but one thing was certain: if this rescue mission went down, there would not be a man in uniform in the entire USA who would not know it had failed.

The US military was taking no chances. And the big hitters of US fighter aviation were lined up en masse to accompany Skinny, Spanky, and the other guys, all the way to the Sabray field.

As befits one of the most high-profile rescue operations of the Afghan War, there was an accompanying air-to-ground battle fleet riding shotgun for the Pave Hawks. It consisted of a formation of Boeing AH-64 Apache attack helicopters, with their 30-millimeter cannons and Hellfire missiles.

By 2005, this fast, maneuverable, heavily armed gunship had become the scourge of a thousand Middle East terrorists. It was the most feared attack aircraft among insurgents everywhere. Its highly skilled two-man crew fires a laser-guided missile that essentially cannot miss.

The crew rides in tandem with the pilot, behind and above the copilot-gunner. Both men can open fire independently. Their aircraft is powered by two General Electric T700 turbo-shaft engines with high-mounted exhaust.

The Apache AH-64 cruises at 180 miles per hour and is designed to sustain hits from 23-millimeter rounds. The airframe includes 2,500 pounds of fuselage protection, and its fuel system is self-sealing to thwart ballistic missiles. In addition, it has a standard of crashworthiness unmatched by any combat helo—in particular, its landing gear and pilot seats, all designed to absorb the impact of a crash landing.

Apache pilots usually fly into a frontline environment, with their M230 chain gun "slaved" to their helmets, forcing the gun to track head movements and aim precisely where the pilot looks.

As for the air-to-surface Hellfire missile, a five-foot-long antitank killer armed with twenty pounds of high explosive, this precision rocket makes nearly a thousand miles per hour through the air.

The legendary US four-star general Carl Stiner, former commanding general of the Eighty-Second Airborne, and C-in-C US Special Forces, was a Tennessee farmer by birth, and there was nothing he didn't know about straight shooting. Said the general, "You could fire that Hellfire missile through a window, from four miles away, at night."

Also flying with them would be the A-10 Thunderbolt II, an unlovely but supremely effective single-seater fixed-wing, a specialist in close air support. This monster carries the heaviest automatic cannon ever mounted on a US fighter aircraft: the GAU-8 Gatling-type Avenger 30-millimeter rotary. It fires big shells, depleted uranium, armor-piercing, if required, at four thousand rounds per minute.

It's a bit slow to warm up. When the pilot hits the button, it unleashes "only" fifty rounds in the first second—and sixty-five to seventy thereafter—and is sufficiently accurate to put 80 percent of its shells inside a forty-foot circle from a distance of four thousand feet, in flight; slant range: four thousand feet in a 30-degree dive.

When this tiger of a fighter plane comes lumbering over the horizon, best tighten your sandals and run for your life. The A-10 can also loiter in the sky for an extended time at altitudes lower than a thousand-foot ceiling, typically flying relatively slowly—at 350 miles per hour—in readiness for its ground-attack role. Fast fighter-bombers find it almost impossible to match the A-10's ability to get a fix on slow-moving targets and then strike hard, with devastating accuracy.

Additionally, it can get off the ground from short, rough landing strips, even under a heavy load. In a pinch, the old Thunderbolt can take off from a damaged air base runway or even down the middle of a highway. It's a tough, sturdy, go-anywhere airborne warrior, and when the pilot opens up with that Gatling cannon, watch out.

When racing in to support US ground troops, the A-10 Thunderbolt pilots have a telling motto: Go ugly early.

A giant aerial refueling tanker accompanied the group, and flying way above the formation was a Lockheed AC-130 Spectre gunship, a heavily armed ground attack specialist. Its Vulcan and Bofors cannons are all ranged on the port side of the aircraft, which allows it to make a large circle around a target, and continue with sustained fire for longer than almost any other gunship.

The AC-130 Spectres became Afghan specialists in very short order after they first arrived in 2001. With so many Taliban and Al Qaeda strongholds dug into the mountains, they were the natural US attack platform and saw service in all the major assaults in the early part of the war. These included missions in Kandahar, Tora Bora, and Operation Anaconda, which was fought in the Shahi-Kot Valley, due south of Kabul, in March 2002.

The AC-130 requires a crew of thirteen, including five officers: pilot, copilot, navigator, and fire control and warfare officers. Among the eight enlisted men, there are a flight engineer, TV operator, infrared detection operator, loadmaster, and four aerial gunners.

The aircraft is almost 100 feet long, with a 130-foot wingspan. Power plant: four turboprops, five-thousand-shaft horsepower each. Maximum takeoff weight: seventy tons. It's feared by enemy militants as much as the Apache gunship, because once that Spectre gets its range, it's basically time for prayers.

The Lockheed gunship has one more priceless asset: its giant infrared spotlight, which is completely invisible to the naked eye but crystal clear to everyone wearing night goggles. At the precise moment of rescue, that spotlight will come lasering through the night air and illuminate the landing zone for Skinny to slam down the glow stick, hopefully straight over home plate.

The US High Command was taking no chances on this one, top secret as it was, with half the military world waiting to hear that Marcus was safe, and that the bodies of his close buddies Danny, Axe, and Mikey had been located and gathered up. No level of US heroism in this entire conflict had ever been edged more cruelly with such a deep and abiding sadness.

The air armada that would accompany the two Pave Hawks thundered off the runway with as little fuss as possible shortly after 2100. It regrouped high over the foothills east of the base and then flew in the agreed-upon formation straight up to the Hindu Kush. Its mission: to soften up (read: frighten the living daylights out of) the Taliban on the mountain.

"I was well aware of the route we were taking," Chris Piercecchi said later. "We were headed into the exact same valley as before—the one where they fired and missed once, and then smashed a missile into the Chinook. It might not yet have been real for everyone, but it was sure as hell real for me, right from the start."

Checky, of course, would be the first man out of the aircraft, if necessary, down a rope in the night to grab Marcus. He would also be the first man to come under fire if the big boys hadn't yet wrapped up the Taliban.

At 2200, the final signal came into both cockpits. The rescue mission was a go. Engines running, rotors flashing in wide circles, doors slammed. Outside, an unusual number of the guys stood alongside the runway to watch the takeoff. It was as if everyone was involved in this rescue, if not physically, then with their fighting hearts and steel-rimmed willpower. There was not a man among them who would not have grabbed a rifle and gone with them if such a call had come.

Skinny led the way, climbing into the night sky, tracked by the second Pave Hawk. Below them, a thousand eyes watched the helos clattering higher and higher, up toward the black canyon where death lurked on every escarpment.

Alongside the runway, men who had faced fire and fury in battle together just offered those tight little nods, one to the other. Everyone understood the stakes. And no one spoke, except for one Navy SEAL chaplain, standing alone. He just muttered, "God go with you."

The rescue helicopters kept going, following behind the support fleet of Apache gunships, the A-10 Thunderbolts, and the Spectre, which was flying far higher than the rest. But once more the cloud cover was heavy, and the pilots did not even get much help from the mountain peaks below, which, on this ride, usually got whiter and whiter the farther north they traveled.

Tonight there was little in the way of guidance from the outside. Everything was concentrated on the instrument panels in the cockpits—altitude, speed, direction, GPS numbers, all communications—while the pilots peered through their NVGs at a green world that was growing dimmer by the mile, the moon and the stars obliterated by the dense cloud.

After a half hour, the Pave Hawks were in contact with the main fleet. They could see the lights when they ventured above the clouds, but that was not a good plan. They needed to stay low, reducing the enemy's ability to see them, creeping along the valley floors, staying close to the mountain wall. Because there, Taliban radar, if any, would find it impossible to pick them up. There's nothing like a zillion tons of solid granite stretching to the sky to confuse even the most sophisticated radar beams.

Skinny and Spanky sped on along the main river valley, preparing for the final approach, as close to the mountain wall as it was possible to fly. High above them the clouds were shrouding the mountains and blocking out all light from the stars.

The trouble was that the LZ was much higher than the route they were now following, and they needed to ascend very soon. Meanwhile, with so many people shouting, communications were becoming slightly chaotic.

Everyone wanted to know the same thing: "What's the status? Over." "What's the status?" "What's the status?" Since no one could see a damned thing beyond the cockpit glass, it was a hard one to answer.

Both rescue pilots began to climb swiftly, like two dragonflies, against the massive cliff face. And right there, they could see a new sight: green flashes through their goggles, like the center of a major thunderstorm. But this was not one of nature's spectacular sights—this was heavy-duty American firepower slamming into that mountain, making doubly sure that no member of the Taliban army got even a half shot at a US plane. And certainly no heavy machine gun fire aimed at Marcus Luttrell, wherever he might be.

The policy was simple: blitz that mountain until it goes quiet. Real quiet.

Mohammed Gulab, on the ground with Marcus, up against the wall, heard the American air attack coming in from miles away, right out of the west, above the cloud cover. They were about ten miles away when he first heard them. And, almost simultaneously, he again saw white lights moving on the mountain, a sure sign that Shah's army was about to have one last crack at either killing him and Marcus or bringing down a US fighter aircraft with a missile.

At this point, all options were narrowing. They all knew the rescue team was scheduled to make the pickup, and therefore the distant roar of those aircraft had to be associated with that operation. From where Gulab sat against the fieldstone wall with Marcus, a counterattack by the Taliban seemed imminent.

He stood up and hissed to his American friend, "Marcus! Marcus! Lights. Taliban!" And he pointed over to the slopes on the opposite side of the village, where the activity was now more obvious.

The American commanders moved very quickly, ordering everyone to his feet and over the wall. The other side had a bigger drop and would provide much more protection.

Problem: Marcus could not make it by himself. So Gulab grabbed his rifle, heaved that over there, and then called in Norzamund and another friend to help with the wounded SEAL. They had to get him undercover without half killing him with the agony of that shattered left thigh, which was still bleeding intermittently.

Slowly, they lowered him down from the top of the wall, but the American was so exhausted fighting the pain, trembling with the effort, that Gulab went for the only answer there was. He took the rifle, leaned it on top of the wall, a nice height, and aimed it straight up the mountain at the Taliban lights.

By now, his warning had been heeded by everyone, and the "Green Berries" opened fire immediately. Marcus produced his telescopic glass and began "spotting": guiding the fire and keeping Gulab's aim steady, focused on the precise positions of the enemy.

Gulab says he'd had other spotters in battle, but never one as good as Marcus. Despite the Texan's pain, he never lost concentration and kept calling the shots, via hand signals, with the calm accuracy of a real professional. Gulab just kept firing, blowing out the distant lights whenever he could.

It seemed like only seconds later when the American battle fleet came rumbling over the mountain, and it launched an air-to-ground attack the likes of which the tribesmen had never seen before.

The US air fleet hit that mountain with everything it had. And it may have been just his imagination, but Gulab thought he saw great mountain oaks literally lifted out of their roots and flung skyward. The glare from the bomb blasts illuminated the land, and there were huge spouts of earth erupting into the air, along with bodies, weapons, and heaven knows what else.

The Apache helicopters were circling around and around, strafing the ground with cannon fire and unleashing those ferocious Hellfire missiles, all of them leaving fiery trails before the blasts. Just above them were two fixed-wing fighter-bombers slamming rocket after rocket into the forest area, reducing Sabray's prime forestry to splinters.

Gulab watched all of this merciless destruction with a mixture of "Praise Allah for our deliverance" and the most profound sadness. He had seen pictures of the end of World War II, and shocking photographs of cities in Poland, of desolate streets turned to rubble, of shell-shocked people standing in front of their shattered homes. The tears, and the heartbreak, and the decimation of their dreams. Sad. Inconsolable. Ruined lives.

Those were his feelings as he watched the greatest power on this earth smash its high explosives into his family's lands. He was aware that the Americans meant only to help—to them, those steep mountain acres were of no consequence. They were just the tribal lands of a people that Washington, DC, scarcely knew existed.

But to some, however, they were everything. It was upsetting to watch that earlier daytime bombing raid, which blew off a few roofs. But this was entirely different. This nighttime raid featured the most formidable air-to-ground weapons in the US arsenal. It would have leveled a medium-sized city.

At the time, there was a stampede among the women and children back up the hill to their homes, to seek protection from the onslaught.

Gulab had sheltered his wife at his father's house because it was plain that she and the children could not go to their own home. With Marcus and Gulab gone, that would be the Taliban's first stop, for some kind of mass slaughter of the innocents.

Their land, their trees, just being systematically smashed. It was bad. And Gulab was unsure whether he should recount his unhappiness to Allah. He was, after all, doing His bidding, and he'd tried to obey Him in every way. And the object of the holy instructions was still there, standing beside him, signaling the line of fire, as the tribesman blasted away with an American Special Forces rifle.

Marcus himself, according to Gulab, had a slight smile on his face as the American fighter pilots finally pulverized the Taliban army. He seemed oblivious to the shattering noise and the thunder of the explosives. He just looked like a man who'd been waiting a long time for this moment, and, despite his pain, despite everything, he was gazing out over the opium field with some satisfaction.

The terrorist troops taking the airborne shellacking were the exact same tribesmen who had tried over and over to blow him up and gun him down; the same men who had killed all three of his friends. That smile of his was very obviously grim in nature. But amidst all the chaos, it was still the smile of a real warrior.

The two Pave Hawks continued their climb up toward the level of the landing zone, leaving the dark river valley far below. The scenario was unaltered, everyone demanding to know the status all across the airwaves, while the US fighters were still hurling everything they had against the Taliban.

And then, quite suddenly, that all stopped, and the Taliban were temporarily silenced. But then the target changed. And as Skinny and Spanky straightened up for the homestretch, leveling out for their final approach, the US air attack switched from ground targets to unknown expanses of the mountain wall.

The objective was now very different. It was simply to make as much noise as humanly possible, to drown out the noise of the helicopter rotors and, hopefully, to deceive the Taliban missile men as thoroughly as possible. Hellfire missiles slammed into the granite walls of the mountain from every angle.

But the clouds were still completely uncooperative, cloaking the range in a fogbound mantle of thick, gray mist. Visibility: close to zero with the naked eye. And in the middle of all this came a curveball out of nowhere: from home base, a last-minute two-kilometer correction in the coordinates was coming in over the radio.

This meant the pickup point was now a mile and a quarter different. Most of the aircrew thought this was a darned fine time to be telling them, with the two rescue aircraft hurtling in toward the landing zone, the final approach for Spanky. Worse yet, the navigators had only the numbers, with nothing to inform them whether they represented a sheer cliff face or the valley floor.

Mass confusion from HQ, but no earthly point charging ahead to the wrong place, somewhere where Marcus wasn't. Gonzo, Spanky's copilot, was very shaken by this.

"I just cannot tell the guys inside this aircraft to get that done fast enough!" he yelled.

Skinny's copilot, Major John Phalon, said later, "It was the time—

there was almost none left—even with my helmet on, I was pulling out what little hair I still had!"

But Colonel Skinny was certain. And he snapped out a command: "These new coordinates have to go in—let's get it done right now."

And still there was no moon and nothing from the stars. It was getting darker, not lighter. And then—horrors—their NV goggles began to shut down. There was no light to magnify. Their only chance was the infrared camera, a small screen relaying the residual heat from the rocks below.

The performance of the commander, Skinny Macrander, was sensational. He was out in the lead, flying to the right, racing as close as possible to the mountain wall, on his side. You couldn't pay guys to do that in the light, never mind the pitch-dark.

He said later that he was just doing the best he could. But it was more than that. It was nothing short of brilliant, an exhibition of ice-cold military flying, which had a special private glory of its own.

And right now they began to see the scale of the operation they were in. The valley floor around Sabray was electric with infrared marker strobes: sharp bright pulses visible only through night vision goggles. Every Ranger, every aircraft in the sky, was flashing an identifying warning in this way: *Don't shoot over here, for God's sake, you'll hit me!*

And at this point, Spanky elected to make some high-speed maneuvers designed to confuse the Taliban. He started banking and swerving at low level, and then he got another shock. It instantly became obvious that the air was much thinner up here, and the massive rotors were not getting as much lift.

The Pave Hawk was too heavy, and the only way to lighten her was to dump fuel. The crew went right ahead and unloaded the weight, but instantly there was another nightmarish development: the infrared Nightsun system on board the Spectre gunship could not penetrate the dense cloud cover. The system shut down, and now the landing zone could not be illuminated.

This was a five-alarmer. And the comms chief in the Spectre screamed the warning: "ALOs! . . . Negative burn! . . . Negative burn!"

The landing zone was now in total darkness. Spanky was desperate, still searching for the light that wasn't there. He and Colonel Skinny were in close communication, but they couldn't see a thing. In this, the most high-profile rescue mission the US Air Force had mounted for years, both lead pilots were flying blind, surrounded by mountains.

And then this weeklong saga of divine interventions produced its next inexplicable miracle.

The A-10s were just organizing one last concerted attack on the Taliban hillside, when the rear gunship quite suddenly spotted a gap in the cloud cover. He reacted with devastating speed, banked, and gunned the eleven-ton straight-wing aerial brawler straight at it, slamming on his targeting laser and lighting up the landing zone like a theater spotlight on a Bolshoi ballerina.

Gonzo saw it and accepted that he was in the clear presence of a miracle.

Spanky, too, was incredulous. "It was a sudden bright beam—

seemed like from nowhere—and in all of these hundreds of miles, it was exactly where I wanted to land."

Said a wide-eyed Major Gonzo, "It was like the finger of God, out of the darkness, aimed straight at the landing zone."

The aircrew could now actually see where they were coming in. And a few of them nearly went into shock. This was no football field; no wide, flat pasture. This was a narrow shelf hacked into the side of the mountain below the village. It could not have been more than sixty feet wide, and from the open door of the Pave Hawk, it looked like about three feet.

Sergeant Checky, who was sitting in the doorway, could not believe it. Later he said, "This was a landing zone I can state no pilot would even consider landing on in daylight. It was hard up against the mountain wall, and it was pitch-dark."

At the time he just gulped and muttered, "It's pretty small." And then, "*You mean we're gonna land there?!*"

Up front in the lead helo, Colonel Skinny rapidly lost height and set the helicopter to come in regardless of the flying bullets. It seemed that the surviving Taliban on the hillside had made their decision and were banging away at the opium field, determined to make life as difficult as possible for the Americans, trying to turn the LZ into a death trap that might drive away the rescue helicopters.

Skinny kept coming, getting ready to drop that glow stick exactly in the middle of that flat ground. And down below, Marcus was calling the shots to Gulab and the Rangers gunners, staring through the glass, directing the fire, watching the remaining lights on the hillside.

He was trained for this, and never had he been more determined to outwit an enemy.

In came the lead Pave Hawk, engines howling, into the hail of Kalashnikov gunfire, bullets pinging off the fuselage. A grim-faced Colonel Skinny dropped that glow stick dead center in the LZ, and then ripped open the throttles and banked away steeply, climbing up the face of the mountain at a lunatic angle, trying to draw Taliban fire.

This was mission critical, the tactic designed to offer irresistible bait to the Taliban, tempting them to aim at Skinny's aircraft. He knew he might get hit again, and this time hit badly, but he never flinched. At least, not so that anyone noticed. And when he finally drove the lead Pave Hawk away over the valley, the air above the zone was clear and lit brightly by Skinny's glow stick.

Right then, Major Spanky Peterson turned toward the landing zone, hoping nothing more could go wrong, and steered the Pave Hawk toward Gulab's mountain. He came in at an angle, intending to swing onto the flat ground with a slow descent and land on the flattest part he could see. It was, however, with mounting dread that he realized exactly how narrow it was.

Straight ahead was the mountain wall. Directly below the helicopter was a drop of probably two thousand feet straight down. The margin for error was just about zero. It was, without a doubt, the most dangerous landing he had ever seen.

One thought dominated his mind: *If the rotors catch that mountain wall, even by a half inch, well, that's all she wrote.*

There was, however, one other thought in his mind: *failure unthinkable.*

Right next to him, Lieutenant Gonzo had his hands tight on the throttles, ready to go immediately to emergency lockout—a last resort if a sudden surge of power is required.

The tension in the Pave Hawk was atomic, every noise and almost every thought drowned out by the roaring, shuddering beat of the big main rotor—that familiar *Bom! Bom! Bom!*—as the crew strained to see through the weird glow from Skinny's firework illuminating the ground. This was high alert gone mad.

They were ten feet from touchdown, and Spanky was hovering and losing height in slow motion. The navigator was counting, the aircraft lurching in sudden gusts of mountain wind.

"Seven . . . six . . . five . . . four . . ." And then it happened: someone had miscalculated the depth of the loose earth and sand on the opium field, and those fifty-four-foot-wide rotor blades suddenly scooped up the dusty ground into a seething, blinding vortex— a sandstorm that enveloped the aircraft and rose thirty feet into the air. It billowed over the entire area. No one could see a thing.

"Brownout!" shouted the navigator.

With the rotors screaming, Spanky held tight over the narrow land, neither rising nor falling. But the situation was worse than dangerous. This was dire. There was no landmark, nothing to take a fix, impossible to see the drift, if any, and beyond the cockpit glass swirled an unimaginable dust storm.

The downwash of the rotors was whipping it higher. They were enveloped in a churning, choking cloud of brown dust. A landing was not just impossible, it could prove lethal, and the commander immediately understood he was in the helicopter pilot's worst nightmare: flying in the mountains, confined space, pitch-dark, no visual reference point. Even the lights on the LZ had died in the dust.

The pilot does, of course, have instruments to show the drift of the aircraft. But this felt like flying with your eyes closed. The enormous danger was stark in Spanky's mind:

If we drift and then touch down on an uneven surface, we will most likely roll over, because the first wheel becomes a tipping point. That's disaster. And in a brownout, it's impossible to see whether we're drifting left or right. You basically need to know just one truth: if the blades touch the ground, she breaks up.

No one in the Pave Hawk's crew had ever experienced anything this dangerous before. Spanky held the bird, and his nerve, with iron control, and everyone braced for a blind touchdown. Maximum alert.

Lieutenant Gonzo suddenly got a sight of the rock face, and he called it: "Mountain wall fifteen feet from rotors!" To himself, he muttered, "Holy crap! If we bump that way, we're gonna hit it!"

Next to him, Spanky suddenly saw through the dust cloud the two-thousand-foot drop, gulped, and told himself, *If we drift on touchdown, we will crash.*

Lieutenant Gonzo said firmly, "If you guys believe in prayer, you might want to pray right now."

Sergeant Checky recalled, "I knew the only thing that might save you in a helicopter crash was to get down flat on the floor. I figured at that point we're gonna hit—we're gonna crash." And the big staff sergeant hit the deck:

"Stop left! . . . Stop right! . . . Stop left!"

The pilot was completely dependent on directions from his crew and could do nothing but hover, blind in the dust. And then finally there was a call from the rear gunner: "We're two and a half feet from a couple of trees! Stern rotor!"

Spanky knew which way was front and which way was back, and he edged forward, still hovering in the dust cloud.

"If you've a nice calm person in the back," says Checky, "someone just calling 'Come a little left,' that's one thing, and you make the correction. But when everyone's yelling 'Stop right!' 'Stop left!' then that's different, and I guess you react best you can."

Spanky lifted slightly and edged right, to avoid the looming terror of the mountain wall.

Gonzo dived for the duel controls to stop the pilot from overcorrecting. It was a possible overcorrection that worried the lieutenant, and he held on, talking to Spanky calmly, ensuring that there were no drastic, heavy moves.

But Spanky was too experienced for that, and he was just looking for anything on the ground that wasn't going to blow away. But he couldn't see anything. Only the brownout cloud, which was still swirling, still blocking out all forms of light.

And right here the major understood he might be facing the end.

A couple of feet one side or the other could sound the death knell for everyone aboard.

"I actually knew we were going to crash," he said. "I couldn't stop it. I couldn't see. Somehow I was going to let everyone down. Everything was rolling through my head: the mission, my family, my kids, and the most awful sense of grief, because I just felt all was lost.

"I came here to help Marcus, to get him out, and there's his family as well. And now I'm going to crash and roll down the mountain."

And at that moment, something broke. Through the dust in front of the cockpit, very suddenly there appeared a bush, elevated high, right in front of Spanky's eyes, its leaves rustling in the ferocious wind from the rotors. It gave him, at last, a fix: a left and a right; an up and a down. He couldn't see the ground or anything else, but he could see the bush, and it would keep him straight in the sandstorm.

Not since Moses saw God appear out of the burning bush on Mount Horeb has any shrub, plant, branch, or thicket meant that much to one man. "It saved us," says Spanky. "It was the only thing I had—the only reference. So long as I stayed steady on those rustling leaves and held us motionless above the ground, we would not die. Even if we drifted, I at last had a fix, and I could correct against it."

Very slowly the dust cleared, and when it did, Spanky saw that they were less than two feet from the edge of the cliff. On the other side, the blades were whipping through their enormous circle, slower and then faster, as the beat of the engine rose and fell, thunderous in the night air, probably three feet from the wall.

"I could see the ground by then, and it looked flat. I lowered the

Pave Hawk until the wheels bumped, dead together, and about four of the guys yelled, 'Touchdown!'

"There's a lot of emotion when you cheat death that narrowly," he said. "All the guys had families and loved ones, and we'd all thought we'd probably die.

"I almost went into shock when I fully realized how near we were to disaster. I was pretty sure I would not have done this in Tucson during the day; not touching down on a ledge this narrow, with such total catastrophe on either side. It was just too stupid, too big a risk. I would not have done it. I guess I did it for Marcus."

Once they were down, things began moving very fast.

Gulab's two friends helped Marcus back up and over the stone wall into the opium field where the US helicopter was now stationary, its rotors pounding the air, deafening in the dust. No one really knew what to do. To Gulab, it was like something from outer space; he'd never been in a helicopter.

The light was bad, and Marcus began to walk forward toward his own people. Gulab later said, "It crossed my mind that if the Americans did not know him personally, they might be confused by this big bearded man in Afghan clothes. I held on to his arm, and we walked forward—now two bearded men in Afghan clothes.

"I remembered how confusing it had been when we first struggled up those stone steps in the woodland and found ourselves face-to-face with the Rangers. I, of course, had been shouting loudly the code on Marcus's tattoo: 'Two-two-eight!' It worked then, but I had no idea what to shout now.

"And right then, a big, powerfully built US airman jumped down from the helicopter and walked forward a few paces with his rifle leveled at Marcus's head."

Checky picks up the story:

There was still one hell of a lot of billowing dust, and nothing was real clear. I could see something coming toward us, very indistinct in the dark. Whatever the hell it was, we did not want it anywhere near us, and definitely nowhere near the helicopter.

I knew those Taliban would stop at nothing to take out the rescue Pave Hawk. I just hoped the US Air Force had pounded the hell out of them; slowed 'em right down.

But there were two figures coming toward me. And, of course, none of us knew what Marcus would look like or what he'd be dressed in. I had no idea who these tribesmen were, and a part of my job was to protect the crew at all costs.

The first one's a big guy, and I knew he was not an American because he was coming straight to the helicopter. I had no choice. And I drew my weapon, because at this point, from where I stand, he's a threat. I see the second guy step out behind him—and he's also wearing the Afghan clothes.

Right now I'm thinking, *Jesus! I'm going to have to shoot both of them.* And my finger is on the trigger. I'm one split second from pulling it. But now there's a third guy, stepping out right behind them. And to my eye, this one was American, US military.

I could see he was a Ranger, and he indicated not to shoot, pointing out Marcus and then Gulab. That stopped me from opening fire, but I still needed to run my checks, and I had a couple of questions for Marcus which he must answer.

The first one involved Spiderman. Would you believe? And I called it out to him, "Who's your favorite superhero?"

"Huh?" said Marcus, looking at me as if I'd gone out of my mind. But then he clicked onto the identity procedure, forced a grin, and said the correct answer: *Spiderman*. Identity confirmed.

The PJ gestured for Marcus and Gulab to move into the helicopter, as everyone could see Marcus needed urgent medical attention. But it was a bit more rushed than that. With sporadic gunfire echoing over the mountain, and Taliban small-arms fire zinging into the opium field from their new position a hundred meters away, Checky just shouted the order "Go! Go! Go!" and Gulab dived into the helo, somehow dragging the wounded Marcus behind him.

Spanky had the engines screaming, and the rotors were gathering a whipping speed. Checky leaped aboard, slammed the door tightly shut, and Spanky lifted off, drifting right, and then somehow launching the Pave Hawk straight over the cliff—throttles wide open, the blades cutting into the thin mountain air, but lifting them now, up and away from this terrible place, where they'd come as close to death as any of them ever expected to do.

"For a few seconds I just looked at Marcus," says Checky. "And in that short time, I could see in his eyes what he'd been through: the blood-soaked saga of the original battle, the lifelong hurt at the deaths of his three close buddies. And that was a hurt which would never go away.

"I could see the intensity in his eyes. And I understood that for now he was probably unreachable. The key thing was, we had him out of there, and at last he was safe. I just shook his hand warmly and said, 'Welcome home, brother.' "

Gulab never looked down through the window into the darkness as they flew over his village. He thought it might be the last time he ever saw it. Somewhere down there were his wife and family. Also, it was surrounded by vicious Taliban killers who'd vowed to kill them all.

The experience of riding in a helicopter was new to him: the noise, the lurching action as they swerved through the mountains. Gulab understood that just above their heads was this massive rotor that somehow kept them high. But the thought of the thousand-foot drop below the aircraft floor was unnerving to him.

And he quietly prayed for the mercy of Allah; that He would not allow the Taliban to hit the helicopter. However, he could hear bullets hitting the fuselage as they made their escape. He was not overconfident.

Gulab was clinging to Marcus's arm, sitting on the floor with the other big American—the one with the machine gun; the one who, a few minutes before, looked like he would shoot them both.

There was a major celebration going on in the back of the helicopter, guys whooping and shouting at the triumphant rescue of Marcus. Gulab could tell, for the first time, Marcus was relaxed, back among his own people.

It was quite strange, because he had no idea where they were going. He'd lost all sense of direction, although he did think they were headed south. It was a short ride, but, as ever, he and Marcus were never able to speak, and sign language was impossible in the helicopter. So Gulab didn't know what was happening.

About ten minutes into the journey, they started to descend to the small US air base, at Asadabad, some twenty miles from Sabray.

They came in to land very calmly, with plenty of people awaiting the arrival despite it being the middle of the night. Gulab had never been to the American base south of the city, not even when it was used by the Russian occupying forces in the 1980s. But he quickly understood where they were.

Everyone disembarked, and a quick glance around at the distant hills and mountains confirmed it was Asadabad, the capital city of Kunar Province, way over in the east of the country, and only about eight miles from the Pakistan border, which runs through the Hindu Kush.

In some ways, this is a rather sinister place: a longtime base for smugglers and for insurgents fleeing through the mountains back to Pakistan. It's always been rumored this was the hub of American military intelligence, with a secret presence of officers and agents from the US Central Intelligence Agency.

Almost immediately, a large fuel truck came up to refill the helicopter's tanks, and Marcus was led over to a medical room where a doctor was awaiting his arrival. Despite his terrible wounds and accompanying pain, SEAL 228 insisted on walking. Gulab went with him, and while he waited outside the treatment room, they told him Marcus was flying on to the Bagram base, where he had come from originally.

Gulab had no idea what would happen to him, except that he could not go home. Finally, Marcus came out of the doctor's office and was led back toward the refueled helicopter. No one seemed to know whether Gulab was staying with him or not, but he was told firmly to stay right where he was, and Marcus got on board.

Gulab could see him looking through the glass, and he ran toward him, waving and calling his name. But no one took any notice, and the helicopter took off slowly, leaving him behind. "It felt like a knife had gone through my heart," he says. "For me, it was a separation like no other. My warrior brother, and I might never see him again."

Marcus had no idea this was going to happen. He heard the door slam, and he could see the faithful Gulab outside the cockpit, shouting at him.

"I forced myself up and yelled at the pilot," he says. "I yelled at anyone who might listen, that Gulab must not be left behind.

"I understood the pilot could not hear me, and I was banging on the glass windshield of the helicopter ordering them to go back for the Afghani man who had put his life on the line for me more times than I could remember.

"There was anguish on Gulab's face. I was close to tears myself. But the US military had made up its mind: Mohammed Gulab was going nowhere. They were flying me to the medical unit in Bagram, and he was not coming with me.

"It was one of the most heartrending moments of my life. And I thought about it over and over. We never even had time to say a reasonable good-bye; never even a moment for me to assure him I would take care of him.

"It was devastating for both of us. I never saw Gulab again, for years. And I tortured myself over it. I never stopped thinking about it. How could I? How could anyone?"

After they landed at the gigantic Afghanistan home base, Marcus was treated for his extensive injuries and partly debriefed. The military wanted as much immediate help as Marcus could offer on where to locate the bodies of Mikey, Axe, and Danny.

None of that was very easy for any of the SEALs—that final realization that they were gone. There was also the added complication of the missing body of Matthew Gene Axelson. The search guys could not find him despite accurate GPS numbers from Marcus, which pointed out the exact place where the RPG hit and almost blew them both into oblivion.

Marcus could see on the photographs the place where he had been blasted over the edge and into a hole. But there was, apparently, no sign of Axe.

The helicopter rescue guys went back up there and recovered the remains of Mikey and Danny, who were still lying where they fell. And when the coffins were brought out for the final good-byes at Bagram, they all struggled through the Ceremony of the Ramp. "I never saw more tears on a SEAL base," says Marcus.

The Ramp is the sacred SEAL sacrament, conducted when everyone turns out to pay his last respects to a lost brother, filing through the giant Boeing aircraft, past the coffins draped in the American flag. In this case, past the bodies of two valorous SEALs, Mikey and Danny, the likes of whom Marcus Luttrell did not expect to see again.

The navy chaplain conducting the short service at the top of the Boeing's ramp, asked one final favor from God: to let perpetual light shine upon them. Marcus did not think He'd have any problem with that.

But the problem of the missing Axe remained. And this was a mystery. SEALs never leave anyone alone. At the beginning, and all through BUD/S (basic underwater demotion/SEAL) training, they stay with their swim buddy. They always work as a team.

Ever since President John F. Kennedy established in 1962 what he called a "small, elite maritime force for unconventional warfare," they have sought never to leave a man on the battlefield. Alive or dead.

SPECWARCOM, the national command center of the SEALs, was never going to leave Axe up there. If they had to send five helicopter rescue crews to that mountain every day for a hundred years, they'd do it. They were going to find him.

It was extremely difficult for Marcus because he knew only the precise spot where they were blasted by the grenade. He survived, but he had not been shot five times, like Axe was. "It was inconceivable that he had escaped," says Marcus. "And the Taliban do not habitually touch the bodies of infidels. They tend to empty their Kalashnikovs into their faces."

Marcus advocated going back to Sabray and consulting the Pashtun villagers. As he'd experienced, they knew everything that happened in those mountains.

It was decided to contact Maluk, the village elder, who had walked the message about Marcus being alive to the US base. He was also the elder in two other villages, and the only way to find him was through Gulab.

Marcus felt a sense of guilt at asking him for yet more favors, in light of the US military's apparent heartlessness toward him.

"But I knew the Americans were keeping a close guard on him," he says, "and that they could find him, wherever he was. So once more, I backed the goodwill of Gulab, and once more he did not let us down.

"I advised the military that he would lead them to Maluk. And I was certain the great mountain sage would lead our rescuers to the exact right spot."

Gulab doubts that any Pashtun field commander and mujahideen veteran has ever found himself in a position quite so awkward as his own during the hours after Marcus was lifted out.

Within one day, he was requested to find Maluk, the village elder, and persuade him to walk with the SEAL team back to the scene of the June 28 battle for *Murfeerij*, as well as to accompany Maluk and do what he could to help locate the body of Marcus's friend, Axe.

Gulab felt they had been so dismissive of him at the Asadabad base, giving him no time even to say good-bye to the man whose life he had saved, he was tempted to tell them to find their own way.

However, Gulab knew what the warrior Axe had meant to Marcus, and he understood how upset he was. And he understood the closeness of that family friendship, and that Marcus could not bear the thought of him being left dead on the mountainside, so very far from his home and family.

So Gulab decided to comply. For Marcus. For no other reason. "I would find Maluk," he said, "and return with him to the mountain where the battle had been fought and find Marcus's friend."

In fact, Gulab had much more to do with that expedition to find Axe than anyone has ever known. For obvious reasons, he did not tell any local people, and in the absence of Marcus, he kept it all to himself. Maluk gathered a troop of his men around him, and Gulab did the same.

They walked together from Sabray, each confident of success. There had been much talk of this on the little radios they all had in their homes, and everyone knew where Maluk was going.

Axe had not been injured in the blast that hit him and Marcus. He had taken the impact head-on, and the violent air had blown him across the clearing, but he had not been hit by shrapnel and rock particles. He did, however, immediately become involved in a gunfight, although the Taliban moved his body after he died.

When Maluk led everyone to the correct place, they found that Axe had been buried, at least partially, and there was a rope tied to his foot by which they'd dragged him to his resting place on the mountain.

It was a difficult search operation. Gulab kept trying to warn the

Americans that it was likely the Taliban had buried a booby-trap bomb, either with Axe or near him, and they needed to be very careful. The Americans, however, had a highly sensitive electronic metal detector, and they got in quite close to gather the SEAL up in a body bag while the searchers and guides stayed well back.

As with the others, the Taliban had mutilated his body, and the military had to use DNA to assist with full military positive identification.

Axe had fought on to his dying breath. Like Danny. Like Mikey. When they found that third body, they didn't really need DNA. Axe's remains were written in blood, honor, and courage.

"The body could have belonged to no one else except Matthew Gene Axelson," says Marcus. "But I guess you had to know him personally to understand that fully. My brother Morgan, the toughest man I know, understands. He is unable to hear Axe's name without quickly leaving the room. Even now, eight years later. It's often that way with the bravest of men."

There was a huge sense of relief after they found him, despite all the sadness and all the regrets. A lot of SEALs would have found sleep almost impossible, just at the thought of their brother, up there in the dark, surrounded by hostiles, thousands of miles from home. By himself.

8

TREAD SOFTLY AS I LEAVE YOU

It was a relief to Gulab when the last page of the Marcus saga finally ended, but he was now left not just to pick up the pieces but also to make serious moves to protect his family. The constant threats were not to be taken lightly. They were made by ruthless tribesmen who would stop at nothing to get revenge.

They blamed Gulab squarely for saving the infidel, whom they believed should have been executed. And as a kind of extension, they also blamed him for the dozens of deaths they had suffered in battle. Of course, that had happened before Gulab ever laid eyes on Marcus, but a mere technicality like that did not affect Ahmad Shah and his cutthroats.

As far as they were concerned, Gulab had to pay for these "crimes" with his life, and that included all of his close relations. With enormous sadness, he finally accepted he would have to leave Sabray, his family's home for so many generations.

There were several family members to whom he could entrust the house—if necessary, for years—until it was safe for the family to return. But meanwhile, Gulab needed to find somewhere new where they could live away from the spying eyes of the Taliban army.

This was thoroughly awkward for Gulab, as he was now an obvious friend and ally of so many Americans and an "enemy" of a section of his own Pashtun race. Looking back at the great spread of Afghanistan's history, he may very well be the only Pashtun tribesman ever to find himself in such a predicament.

But he had tried to obey the wishes of Allah, the one and only God, and at no time did he believe he had any choice in the matter. And the great majority of his people in the village accepted that and respected his actions. However, it was not them he was worried about.

It was the minority: Pashtun tribesmen who believed in the warlike rantings of men like Ahmad Shah, who were not scholars, not Imams, and not devoted followers of Islam's many creeds.

In his heart, Gulab believed that everything would be taken care of by the American military. But this was more complicated than he fully understood. For instance, the mere question of a reward for what he had done for Marcus should have been simple.

But tribal law says any such reward for acts of valor or chivalry must be bestowed upon *everyone* in the village. Therefore, a simple reward—money or gifts to the family—was forbidden. The Americans were faced with a thousand technical hitches, because a gift to everyone needed to be something like a new road into the village, or perhaps a generator to bring them their first electricity.

And that meant contractors, capital expenditure, machinery being airlifted in, a labor force, and constant discussions with local tribal councils. The generator would mean deliveries of diesel fuel into a place where no truck could ever reach.

The Americans tried to achieve something, and they did repair much of the village after the Taliban onslaught the night that Gulab and Marcus left. But the Taliban tried to block the US military at every turn, leveling accusations of theft and villainy upon the people of Sabray wherever they could. In a sense, it was all hopeless, which in effect left Gulab and his family out in the cold—in the gravest danger in their own village home.

The American military did make it possible for him to do some work for it, but this entailed being away for weeks at a time. Finally, Gulab accepted that he would have to evacuate and establish a new residence. The glowering presence of Shah's Taliban army around Sabray was just too overwhelming.

He made the journey to Asadabad, across the mountain. No word from Marcus since they'd parted. The Navy SEAL was on the other side of the world now, eight thousand miles away, in that Texas place where there's only one star in the sky.

Judging by his injuries, Marcus was not likely to remain in the military any longer. And although Gulab realized he might be gone forever, he still kept asking the Americans for information about him. But they never revealed anything to him.

The city of Asadabad was marginally safer. It's the capital of Kunar Province, located close to Pakistan's northwestern border. It is built in a valley at the confluence of the two rivers, the Pech and the Kunar, right between two massive escarpments.

Its strength is Camp Wright, a heavily armed US forward operating base, within a couple of miles of the town. It stands guard over the notorious smuggling and insurgent freeway known as the Nawa Pass, the next border-crossing point into Pakistan north of the Khyber Pass.

Camp Wright, a center of military intelligence, is the main base of operations for both the CIA and US Special Ops Forces in the mountainous province.

All of which means that the US security troops keep a very tight watch on the fifty thousand residents of Asadabad. There are constant US patrols driving through its dusty streets. Much of the city is surrounded by high defensive concrete walls, with American observers positioned on the ramparts.

Gulab took a room in Asadabad while he searched for a new home. He had money, but not enough to not work, and went first to evening prayers at the mosque close to the bazaar. There he asked for guidance, and the following morning, he found an apartment in a secure, larger central building and took a lease on it.

From there Gulab made his way back to Sabray, walking much of the way but being driven over the middle five miles by a friend who owned a car. It was growing dark by the time he arrived, but his family and many friends were pleased to see him, and even more pleased that he had found a solution to the dangers at home.

He instructed the family to begin packing. At evening prayers, he talked at length to the Imam, and when darkness fell over the Hindu Kush, he stared at the skies above the mosque and prayed that Allah knew that he, Mohammed Gulab, had done His bidding, and that the American was safe.

Looking back, it was the saddest of evenings as they gathered outside the family home and said their final good-byes. No one knew when they would be able to return, for the Taliban army was still camped in the hills above Sabray, and in the absence of Marcus, their target was this one house now being vacated.

They carried their few possessions in shoulder bags, and Gulab's wife wept as she tried to comfort the four children. They set off down the hill, all alone, leaving behind every single thing they had ever known.

Like all field commanders in these mountains, Gulab realized that darkness was their friend:

Just for the moment. The cloudy skies obscured the moon, and I hoped it would remain that way, since it was almost full, and at these heights, in this clear air, its light was often almost as bright as the sun.

We tried to walk in silence, since we all understood the Taliban would kill us any time we were located. A thousand years of survival instinct had ensured our footsteps were soft, our heartbeats low, and our breathing shallow. We carried no lights, and we made no sound, even though I knew my wife's heart was slowly being broken by this dark and cruel journey.

There were eight miles ahead of us, and we dared not stop. The night was bitterly cold, and the children marched with blankets wrapped around their shoulders. My wife walked bravely behind me, guarding them, and occasionally touching my shoulder in this blackest of nights.

Every instinct I had was concentrated on the land around us. As we made our way down this part of the mountain, the trees grew more dense, and I strained my hearing for the sounds which would betray an enemy: the snap of a twig, the near-silent crush of leaves beneath encroaching footfalls, the whispered commands of a troop leader.

In my right hand, I carried the family Kalashnikov assault rifle, a loaded thirty-round magazine slammed into place, safety catch off. In my pocket, I had two more magazines, and I walked on hair-trigger alert.

I understood there were some adequately competent troops in Ahmad Shah's army, but they were all inexperienced, and, thanks to Marcus and his men, many of them were already dead. *If I'm attacked this night*, I thought, *I'm ready.*

And if any of Shah's men should try to make a name for themselves, they should bear in mind I've been trained for battle and ambush since I was eight years old. They should bear in mind just one fact: I'm still alive, and that was not by luck alone.

Yes, if there are enough of them, they may succeed in killing us. But I'll go to meet my Creator with my arms around my wife and children, and with my courage high. I'll take many Taliban with me, and I'll do so in the name of Allah, the Almighty, the one and only God.

I'd have given a lot to have Marcus with us, even though we'd prob-ably be safe so long as the moon stayed hidden. And so we walked on down the mountain, slowly covering the distance, a steady four-hour march until the little ones really could go no farther.

It was daylight when we finally arrived, and the children were ex-hausted and fell asleep on those big Afghan cushions I'd sent in a couple of days previously. My wife too was extremely tired but in-sisted on going to the market for supplies while I stood guard.

When she returned, Gulab made a recce of the surrounding area, searching for the most vulnerable spots from where an attack might come. For the moment, he was the lone sentry, and he would remain on duty at his post for most of each night, his AK-47 primed and loaded. It was a habit he would never lose.

It was only a week since he had watched Marcus fly away. The American was in Texas by now and probably not suffering any dis-ruptions. Gulab kept thinking he would be in touch, but there was nothing. No news, no communication.

Each day, when he walked in the morning in Asadabad, he stopped to talk to US troops, asking if they could put him in contact with his former houseguest, but no one could. Gulab had the impression they wanted to be rid of him. And, in a way, he understood that—an armed Afghan tribesman in native dress trying to get in touch with a US Spe-cial Forces operator, recently wounded, after a mountain battle with the Taliban army.

It was an unusual situation. And Gulab was running into a constant brick wall of silence. Equally, he had no idea how Marcus could find him, since he had no address or phone number, and was gone from the village.

It seemed they would never see each other again. And if the Taliban ever got into the surroundings of the Asadabad residence, Gulab might not survive. All for a foreign stranger. Only the will of Allah now stood before him as any kind of a reason. But he trusted in Allah.

The full extent of the personal danger was revealed when, six months after Marcus had left, Hajid Moresaleem, one of the village elders, was shot in the chest while he was at prayer in his home. His "crime" was having befriended the American.

And they also came for Gulab.

"One year later," Gulab says, "soon after I left Asadabad on a journey to Tharara, my car was ambushed by the Taliban. They shot the driver as we passed, but the vehicle ran on, and this gave me the chance to break out and race for cover. I had my AK-47 with me, and I made my stand among some rocks, well concealed, my rifle loaded. For some reason, they refrained from following up their initial attack. Sensible move. I'd probably have killed them all."

For Marcus's part, he was haunted by the scene of leaving Gulab behind on the tarmac. It stayed with him for many, many months.

Marcus went to endless trouble to find him, made inquiries all over the place, tried to pass messages, and searched through data. He made call after call, talked to returning friends, anything he could to locate Mohammed Gulab. But there was nothing.

And then in the fall of 2006, Marcus was redeployed with SEAL Team Five to another tour of duty in Iraq, where he was wounded again, this time by a shot in the arm. He didn't return to the United States until the following year, but injuries he had suffered in that June 2005 battle against the Taliban had finally done him in, and he was compelled to retire as a Navy SEAL.

There was a lot of stuff that still hurt, but it was the vertebrae in his back that would forever keep him off active duty. In the months and years to come, Marcus would have twenty operations, and his back still aches.

He could have stayed in the navy. Everyone was great to him. But in the same way that he had never been interested in serving in the surface fleet, he never could have been content at a desk job, even in the command centers of the teams. Even in planning and strategy.

Petty Officer Luttrell joined for the blood and thunder of combat. He's a SEAL, not a tactician, although he probably could have done that. But his heart wasn't in it. And it was the second saddest day of his life when he finally walked out of SPECWARCOM for the last time.

He never stopped searching and thinking about Gulab, but the years 2005 to 2007 were packed with responsibilities and obligations, including all the medical procedures and the publication of *Lone Survivor*. He hardly had time to sit down and take stock of his life.

Marcus continued to seek news of Gulab from fellow SEALs who were near where he heard Gulab might be, but there continued to be no trace of him. Strangely, it was not much different for Gulab. One group of US guards on one of the base camps told Gulab that his American buddy had walked out onto the mountain and committed suicide.

That was when he knew Marcus was alive, because he knew the SEAL would never kill himself. Thus, separated by eight thousand miles of ocean, jungle, and desert, each man conducted his search, one for the other, and got absolutely nowhere.

Finally, a family friend of the Texas beauty who would become Marcus's wife told him he'd found Gulab. He did not wish to be identified, which was surprising, since he's just about the least shy and retiring US Special Forces commander you could meet: a big, boisterous Green Beret named Joe, who'd located Gulab in Asadabad. He also arranged a cell phone hookup so they could speak—as ever, without understanding one word of what the other was saying, but, in another sense, understanding everything.

This all went on for several months while Marcus tried to find a way to get Gulab into the United States for a visit. For a while, this seemed impossible—the visitor being a full-blooded Afghan tribesman; a devoted Islamist who had fought jihad; a man never seen in Western clothes, only tribal dress, and rarely without his Kalashnikov. Add to that his lack of a birth certificate, never mind a passport, and, indeed, the lack of a birthday.

At first, about seven officials in US Immigration almost went into cardiac arrest. This was not, after all, what you might call orthodox. But Marcus marshaled his Texan network and started a process to have Mohammed Gulab welcomed to the United States. It would take a while, but in the end he "got by with a little help from his friends." Marcus and his friends and family pulled all the strings they could to finally persuade the authorities that Mr. Mohammed Gulab posed no danger to anyone and was indeed a worthy person to visit these golden shores.

Also in 2010, as Marcus was working on bringing Gulab to America, he was reintroduced to another person who played a critical role in his rescue. Marcus was working on his new venture, the Lone Survivor Foundation, the mission of which is to build or acquire comfortable retreat centers in beautiful settings for our wounded service members and their families—places where they may restore their lives, and rebuild their hopes and dreams for the future. Help with the transition to civilian life is offered, plus support and therapeutic expertise, and it comes from people who understand the enormous toll that combat action and overseas deployment can take on a family. Marcus sees the foundation being there for those brave men and women who built a career on sacrifice, dedication, courage, and loyalty, but who suddenly find themselves perhaps in a debilitating personal transformation from life-changing wounds, both physical and mental. The foundation offers assistance in putting that everlasting anguish into context, leaving room in the families for normal life, and for love and hope to flourish once more.

That summer, a fund-raiser for the foundation was held in, of all places, the gigantic parking lot at Minute Maid Park in Houston, home of the Houston Astros baseball team. The main event was a reunion for Marcus, but the military men who helped organize it kept him at arm's length, which he should have known was a bit suspect.

As it happened, they staged one of the greatest shocks of his life, and he's had a few. Right across the city, swooping low, was the unmistakable shape of a twin-turboshaft Sikorsky HH-60 Pave Hawk clattering across the downtown area. It circled and then dropped down toward a plainly designated landing zone, right there in the parking lot. The gathered crowd clapped as it landed, and Marcus watched the pilot climb out and meet the reception committee. They beckoned him to join them, and then he was introduced. Someone said, "Marcus, I'd like you to meet Lieutenant-Colonel Jeff Peterson—'Spanky' to his buddies."

The former SEAL just stood and stared at him, this sensational rescue pilot to whom he owed his life after that death-defying landing in the opium field on that war-torn Afghan night. Marcus didn't even recognize him, but the colonel had seen a few pictures.

He just grinned and said, "Hi, Marcus, how you doing?"

Marcus opened his arms and hugged the pilot "because I didn't have any words to tell him what he meant to me," he said later. "How profoundly grateful I was, and how my heart rate had hit about seven thousand revs per minute as he brought that helicopter down, in a deafening feat of flying, just inches from the cliff face, less from the terrifying drop on the other side."

Once Marcus had composed himself, the colonel showed him the big Pave Hawk he had piloted across downtown Houston, and he pointed out the repainted marks and little dents behind the cockpit.

"That's where they hit us, buddy," he said. "Never stopped us, though."

"You mean this is the actual helo that carried me and Gulab out of there?" Marcus asked in astonishment.

"This is the one," said Spanky. "We thought you might like to see it."

"If I think about it," Marcus said later, "I can still smell the choking brown dust, still hear the thunder of those engines, still feel the shuddering surface of the mountain, the gunfire, the explosions, the tumult, and the shouting.

"No one who was there could ever forget it. And right there in the parking lot, I guess I'd betrayed every emotion I'd felt during the rescue. There was nothing I could do about that. And, on reflection, it was just about all I could offer to a real American hero—a pilot who knew the danger, understood the diabolical risk, but still went ahead and did what he believed was his duty. And all for someone else.

"Those guys from the 920th Rescue Wing: Are they something, or what? And Colonel Spanky and his boss Jeff Macrander—what a team, what a credit to this nation they both are. And their motto still stands before me every day of my life: that others may live."

Money raised that memorable day in the parking lot went immediately toward a beautiful new retreat at Crystal Beach, way down on the scenic Bolivar Peninsula, northeast of Galveston Bay.

Before Gulab could make to it the United States, the Taliban somehow got through the security patrol, burst into his apartment, and took a shot at him. Only one, because Gulab went immediately for his rifle, causing the assassins to flee. But the one bullet ricocheted off the rock wall of the apartment and slammed into Gulab's groin.

Luckily, his wife was close by and gave instant first aid, and they had him in the nearby hospital within twenty minutes. If they had been in remote Sabray, far from a city hospital, things might have been very different.

Eventually they heard at last that Gulab's entry visa had come through, and on a hot August morning, Gulab's plane landed at Houston's George Bush Intercontinental Airport, named for President George H. W. Bush, one of Gulab's real heroes—the man in the White House when the heavy-hitting Reagan Stinger missiles were shipping steadily into the mujahideen mountains.

"My man Joe traveled with him," said Marcus. "And my wife and I just stood there waiting for them to exit customs. It was five years and one month since we'd last met, and the reunion was even more moving than the one I had with Colonel Spanky. When Gulab finally showed up, I just threw my arms around him and hugged him. I remember thanking both this son of Islam and my own God simultaneously for giving me a second chance at life.

"I had a government interpreter, but this was a time when no words were needed between Gulab and me. We each knew what the other was thinking; ten thousand words locked into a couple of big grins. Warrior grins. Me and Gulab had, after all, slugged it out together. We'd always been ready to kick some serious ass, if necessary. That kind of friendship has its own lasting words that need not be spoken."

EPILOGUE

After Gulab and Marcus's brief reunion, complete with a whirlwind tour of Texas and Washington, DC, Gulab returned to Afghanistan. But he was able to come back to the United States later on a six-month visa as an advisor on the *Lone Survivor* movie. In a great turn of events, he was introduced to a new interpreter, Nawaz Rahimi, the son of a very prominent Afghani military officer, Colonel Rahimi Gul Ala-Akbar, who'd trained in Washington and acted as an advisor to the US armed forces. Nawaz is fluent in Pashtun and English, having been to school in the United States, where his family lived for much of the year. His father was revered in Gulab's part of the world, as a former mujahideen officer who'd fought the Russians. Nawaz was the best interpreter Gulab could ever have. He worked for the government, but his knowledge of the language and of the military history of Afghanistan was incredibly valuable. Nawaz has been an incredible asset in helping make this book possible.

Gulab spent many hours wondering if he could live in America. He gazed out at the endless grasses of Texas and could see the prosperity of the ranches and sense the peace. He tried to imagine those vast, flat grazing plains as his home. And sometimes he was successful.

Everyone was kind wherever he went. The question was, could he still find happiness when the cheerfulness was past, and people returned to their own lives, and the novelty of the Afghan tribesman had long departed?

"I agonized over my decision," Gulab says. "Even with all the security of America, I had to go home. I had to go back to my mountains. I had to go back to Afghanistan. But in two little corners of this world, in the Hindu Kush and eight thousand miles away in Southeast Texas, love, respect, and friendship will forever hold Marcus and me together."

Mohammed Gulab

This is Shuryek ridge, high above Sabray, the moonscape where the three goat-herders stumbled upon Marcus, Mikey, Danny, and Axe, and the place where the fate of Operation Redwings was decided.

This is the ever-widening mountain torrent that flows below Sabray down into Kunar River. Mohammed Gulab carried the 250-pound Marcus across this dangerous waterway, twice, when the badly wounded SEAL was unable to walk.

This ancient drystone wall guards the Sabray mosque, the holiest place on the mountain, and where Marcus Luttrell once stood in daily worship with Gulab.

The bright white building on the side of the mountain is Sabray's new mosque—paid for with money sent by Marcus in gratitude after he returned safely to Texas. It serves as a place of Islamic worship and as a place of learning for the local children—"my kids" as the big Navy SEAL often called his youngest friends.

This vehicle, laden with sacks of locally grown rice, waits on the road that Maluk, the Sabray village elder, once walked in order to tell the US base that Marcus was, temporarily, safe. Visitors to Sabray must walk up and over that huge mountain in the background, as the seventy-five-year-old Maluk indeed did.

White clouds finally break over Korangal Valley, which, right here, joins the Shuryek pass. It was somewhere up there that Marcus had his final fall—hundreds of feet down the sheer rockface. Lucky he was a SEAL—anyone else would have been killed by the impact.

ACKNOWLEDGMENTS

The obvious consideration in writing this book was the question of how Mohammed Gulab should sound, the voice of the manuscript. And this was made more difficult by the fact that he speaks not a word of English, and I speak limited Pashtun (zero, that is).

But Gulab is a great deal more than a tribesman. His father was a learned man, and so was his grandfather. He himself is a very respected man in his village, and he becomes more so once you know him. Most importantly, Gulab sees himself not as a tribal foot soldier but as an officer. When I asked him, through our interpreter, what he thought would be his equivalent mujahideen rank if he were in the US armed forces, he replied without hesitation.

"I would be a colonel," he said. "Because I was a commander in the field, and if the mujahideen recalled me, that's where I would begin."

He's a wise and accomplished strategist, and he's proud of the fact that if he were to return to Sabray, he would one day be called to serve as the village elder. He's an authority on Pashtun law and tribal traditions stretching back hundreds of years. And among his own people, he is recognized as such. He's a custodian of a folklore that is ever verbal, and is retained, often without documents, in the hearts and minds of the Pashtun nation.

Thus, there was no question of quoting him as a person struggling for words in English. In his own language, he is plainly erudite. Both his US college-educated interpreter, Nawaz, and his eminent father, Colonel Rahimi Gul, insisted that Gulab's words be translated into fluent English, with correct grammar, as if he were a US Army colonel—an officer and a gentleman.

Mohammed Gulab is a proud and dignified man. His story bespeaks a rare nobility. This book is written to afford him the utmost respect.

A portion of the author's proceeds from *The Lion of Sabray* will contribute to Gulab's mission of finding safety for himself and his family.

INDEX

INDEX

ABOUT THE AUTHOR

Patrick Robinson is the coauthor of the #1 *New York Times* nonfiction bestseller *Lone Survivor*, on which the 2013 blockbuster film starring Mark Wahlberg is based. He is also the author of seven internationally bestselling suspense thrillers, including *Intercept, Diamondhead, To the Death*, and *The Delta Solution*, as well as several nonfiction bestsellers, including the coauthored *New York Times* bestseller *A Colossal Failure of Common Sense: The Inside Story of the Collapse of Lehman Brothers*. He lives in the Cayman Islands and spends his summers on Cape Cod, Massachusetts.